MYTHS & LEGENDS
of the
First World War

MYTHS & LEGENDS
of the
First World War

JAMES HAYWARD

SUTTON PUBLISHING

First published in 2002 by
Sutton Publishing Limited · Phoenix Mill
Thrupp · Stroud · Gloucestershire · GL5 2BU

British Library Cataloguing in Publication Data
A catalogue record for this book is available from the British Library

ISBN 0 7509 2865 4

Typeset in 11.5/15pt Photina.
Typesetting and origination by
Sutton Publishing Limited.
Printed and bound in England by
J.H. Haynes & Co. Ltd, Sparkford.

Contents

Acknowledgements

The author extends particular thanks to Deborah Lake, Philip Hoare and Neil Storey, who kindly agreed to read over the text prior to publication, although any errors in the book are mine not theirs. I am also indebted to Neil Storey for his suggestions and great generosity with regard to illustrations.

Thanks are also due to all the historians and biographers on whose work I have drawn, and to Terence Burchell, Seth Feldman, Taff Gillingham, Tim Godden, Iain Overton, Trevor Pidgeon, Chantal Tremblay, Richard Townsley, Tom Tuerlinckx, John Ward (Canadian Press), John Woolsgrove and George de Zwaan (National Archives of Canada); and in addition to the following institutions: the Tank Museum, Bovington, Cambridge University Library, the National Library of Canada, the National Archives of Canada and PA News Library.

Lastly I must thank my editors Jonathan Falconer and Elizabeth Stone, and the staff at Sutton Publishing.

Although every effort has been made to establish and contact copyright holders, this has not been possible in every case. If I have omitted any individuals or organizations I offer my sincere apologies.

List of Illustrations

Plates between pages 110 and 111.

Introduction

In July 1917, as a million Allied troops floundered in an ocean of mud on the slopes below Passchendaele, a girl of 16 named Elsie Wright and her ten-year-old cousin Frances Griffiths took photographs of one another playing with fairies. The girls lived in Cottingley on the outskirts of Bradford, and often played together in a small wooded creek behind Elsie's home. It was here, so they said, that they encountered the fairies, and captured them on film with the aid of a primitive Midg camera.

In due course news of the photographs spread further afield to cause a national sensation, and were championed by the creator of Sherlock Holmes, Sir Arthur Conan Doyle. However, the powers of deduction and logic invested in his fictional detective were nowhere apparent in his credulous dealings with the Cottingley fairies. The fact that the fairies in the first photograph had been traced from an illustration in the *Princess Mary Gift Book* passed unnoticed, while the modern hairstyles they sported were accepted without question. When it was pointed out that the head of a hat pin could be seen protruding from the chest of a gnome in one of the pictures, Doyle explained it as evidence of the fairy navel, and offered this as proof that the little people reproduced in the same way as humans. The fairies appeared only when the girls were alone, it was reasoned, because only they had the trust of the fairies.

Widespread belief in the reality of the images endured for another 60 years, until Wright and Griffiths finally admitted to the hoax in 1983, at the ripe old age of 82 and 76 respectively. In 1917, Elsie Wright had been earning money by colouring sepia photographs of troops and wartime scenes, and at the age of 16 displayed a marked talent for manipulating images – and people – far beyond her years. With the benefit of hindsight it scarcely seems credible that at the height of a war of rapidly developing technologies – submarines, aircraft, tanks, chemical warfare, the internal combustion engine – a sizeable percentage of the population was prepared to believe in the reality of winged little people. Then again, the myth set in motion by Elsie Wright has something in common with the equally supernatural appearance of bowmen and angels on the Retreat from Mons in 1914, and a divine white helper on the battlefields of the Western Front the following year.

The myths and legends spawned during the First World War are legion, and several still manage to excite controversy today. More colourful, if not more numerous, than those of the Second World War, they are fascinating both in their own right and when viewed in their wider historical context. In this study, the first of its kind, I have chosen to examine them in approximately chronological order. The earliest of these legends were essentially innocent in nature and intent: the Angel of Mons, the Russians in England and the Comrade in White all retailed attractive, soft propaganda at a time when the conflict was not going well for the Allies. Other early war myths, such as the Europe-wide spy mania and the reports of atrocities in Belgium, affected both sides in equal measure, and in Britain only assumed the darker hue of hate propaganda after the spring of 1915. This followed a run of German 'frightfulness' which included the first use of poison gas on April 22nd, the sinking of the *Lusitania* early in May, and the mythic crucifixion of a Canadian soldier near Ypres. Perhaps the most infamous atrocity myth, which held that Germany had built a corpse rendering factory near Coblenz in order to extract useful fats from dead soldiers, was concocted by British agencies at about the same time, but not released into circulation until two years later.

While 1915 provided a bumper harvest for the myth makers, thereafter no truly new myths and legends emerged. The corpse factory falsehood of 1917 had already been on the shelf for two years, while the appearance of 'peace angels' over the Thames at

Thurrock in August of the same year was little more than an echo of
the visions at Mons. The myth of the Hidden Hand, a direct ancestor
of the political conspiracy theories common today, was itself an
extension of a particular strand of the general spy mania, and no
more rational than the stoning of dachshunds in 1914. Most of the
other myths discussed in this book – the charge that all British
generals were butchers and bunglers, the notion that tanks won the
war – are postwar creations, and as such are discussed in isolation.
Plainly folkloric trench tales, such as that of the elusive officer spy,
or an outlaw band of deserters in No Man's Land, have little
significance beyond their value as a good yarn, and are mentioned in
passing rather than analysed in detail.

Myths are created, and believed, for many different reasons. The
Angel of Mons and the Comrade in White contained a strong
religious element, and, judging from the variants seen from the
spring of 1915 onwards, were clearly promulgated by church-
affiliated sources, the message being that God was on the side of the
Allies and lending active support. The corollary was that the
Germans were Godless and an enemy of Christianity, this being
manifest in the alleged crucifixion of Belgian and French civilians in
1914 and a Canadian soldier the following year. Certain serving
troops also claimed to have witnessed these various apparitions and
events, but few if any were prepared to say so openly, or on oath,
and therefore their accounts lack credibility. As the writer Trevor
Wilson concluded in *The Myriad Faces of War*, the craving for the
belief that some force, earthly or supernatural, would always be to
hand to snatch victory from the jaws of defeat probably underlies the
credence attached to the story of the Mons angels, or the Russians in
England en route to France with snow on their boots. It may also
explain the fanciful but widespread belief that Lord Kitchener had
not gone down with HMS *Hampshire* in June 1916, but was instead
removed to a secret hide-out, from where he was devising a master-
stroke that would end the war.

A related craving was the desperate need for news from the Front,
at a time when wives, mothers and other anxious relatives found
scant comfort in the terse platitudes of the Field Service Post Card,

and while war reporting in the press was heavily censored. In these circumstances it is hardly surprising that credulity was heightened. This state of affairs was partly responsible for the explosion of interest in spiritualism and clairvoyance, which in turn provided ample opportunity for exploitation of the worst kind. For example, in the case reported as *Davis v Curry*, a police agent named Gardner exposed the fraudulent practice of a medium named Mary Davis, who worked from premises in Regent Street:

> On April 30th 1917, Miss Gardner told Davis that she had been married a few months ago and had been in the habit of hearing every week from her husband, who was in the Essex Regiment, but that, not having heard for the past three weeks, she had been anxious. Davis asked if the witness had been to the War Office, and, hearing that she had not, asked for something which belonged to her supposed husband. Davis then said: 'I can see him – full of life – rushing on with several others. He's not exactly good-looking, but has a pleasing face. He falls amongst others.' Gardner asked: 'Is he wounded?' Davis replied: 'I cannot tell, but he is in bed. I cannot tell where, but it is a pretty place with trees and water; and you will be with him there soon.' Davis told Gardner that her fee for this interview was ten shillings and sixpence, and this was paid.

Astonishingly, Mr Justice Darling ruled that where a medium could offer evidence which indicated a subjective but honest belief in the reality of their own supernatural powers, and had not intended to deceive, this constituted a valid defence. This perverse decision was reversed three years later, and Darling's doubtful professional abilities are examined in more detail in Chapter Seven, in the context of the celebrated Pemberton-Billing libel trial. Yet if by October 1917 a senior judge in the King's Bench Division found it within his gift to dignify crook spiritualism, it is small wonder that a significant percentage of the population at large was credulous regarding angels, fairies, mysterious clouds, secret homosexual conspiracies and a host of other falsehoods.

Hate propaganda gave rise to an entirely different set of myths. The march of the German army through Belgium in August 1914 immediately threw up tales of atrocities on both sides, in which the invaders claimed to have been subject to 'unlawful' attacks by civilians and *franc-tireurs*, while the invaded retailed a catalogue of looting, arson, pillage – and worse. At first, a degree of scepticism prevailed in Britain. In the wake of the veritable epidemic of alleged German 'frightfulness' in the spring of 1915, however, the report of the government-appointed Bryce Committee appeared (and has since been described as an atrocity in itself). Published by HMSO, the Report retailed at one penny (the price of a newspaper), and offered the public a lurid litany of bestial rape, sadistic mutilation and violent murder, in which outrages against women and children predominated. The fact that the Bryce Report bore the stamp of official approval meant not only that such falsehoods were now readily accepted by the public worldwide, but also that two years later the world was ready to believe the deliberate fiction of a German corpse rendering factory. Most Allied atrocity propaganda was discredited soon after the end of the war, adding further to a widespread sense of disenchantment with clergy, politicians and the fourth estate – the latter pair memorably described as 'Junkers' and 'Yellow Pressmen' by the poet Siegfried Sassoon. Nevertheless, the corpse factory myth would not be properly laid to rest by the British Government until 1925.

The most persistent myth of the Great War – that of inept military leadership – only entered into wide circulation several years after the Armistice. In 1927 a junior officer from the Royal Army Service Corps named Peter Thompson published a book titled *Lions Led by Donkeys*, which purported to show 'how victory in the Great War was achieved by those who made the fewest mistakes'. The book is prefaced by an Apologia, which states that 'the words that form the title on the cover of this book were used early in the war, at the German Great Headquarters, to denote the English'. Thompson provided no evidence to authenticate this claim, but it is likely that his otherwise obscure book inspired the historian Alan Clark to attribute the phrase 'lions led by donkeys' to General Ludendorff, the German Chief of General Staff. The pithy appraisal was certainly applied to French commanders after the Franco-Prussian War of 1870, but its use by Ludendorff or any other German general is apocryphal at best. However, thanks to Thompson and Clark, the iconography of the Donkeys has stuck fast in modern memory, despite the fact that the simplistic depiction of all British generals as butchers and bunglers, from Field Marshal Sir Douglas Haig down, is one of the most damaging falsehoods to emerge from the conflict.

Indeed the longevity of such myths almost beggars belief, and makes a nonsense of Sophocles' dictum that a lie never lives to be old. As long ago as 1928, the author and MP Arthur Ponsonby established beyond reasonable doubt that the Kaiser had never once described the British Expeditionary Force as a 'contemptible little army', and that the epithet was in fact coined by the British army itself to swell patriotic indignation. In this it succeeded famously. Yet like the apocryphal lions and donkeys, the legend of the Old Contemptibles has batted on in the history books long after time was declared. It became too ingrained, and too attractive, to discard.

Another factor which boosted belief in myths and legends during the First World War was the impact of new technologies on the popular consciousness. Here the Zeppelin provides a paradigm. German airships were known to be capable of remaining in the air at high altitude for over 24 hours, could cover distances of up to 900 miles, and prior to the outbreak of war had carried thousands of passengers. Little wonder, then, that in Britain in 1914 they were the subject of much exaggeration, mystique, sensationalism – and genuine fear. This, the first fully industrialized war, saw the début of new and startling innovations such as poison gas, submarine warfare and tanks, which to the general public seemed like science-fiction made real. With no radio or television, and with newspapers heavily censored until the summer of 1915, basic facts were hard to come by, and so myth and rumour filled the gaps. It is likely, too, that certain 'innocent' myths and legends represented a conscious, escapist reaction against the scientific and political complexities of the age. Just as the essence of effective propaganda is simplification, so angels, bowmen, protective clouds and white helpers all offered unsophisticated yet unanswerable truths for those who preferred to look backwards to a spiritual Golden Age wherein faith could be placed in older, higher, supernatural powers.

It is ironic that Arthur Machen, the man at once responsible for creating the legend of the Angel of Mons while remaining its most implacable critic, should have continued to find merit in wilfully mystical myth-making. Writing in 1915 he observed:

> The war is already a fruitful mother of legends. Some people think there are too many war legends, and a Croydon gentleman – or lady, I am not sure which – wrote to me quite recently telling me that a particular legend, which I will not specify, had become the 'chief horror of the war.' There may be something to be said for this point of view, but it strikes me as interesting that the old myth-making faculty has survived into these days, a relic of noble, far-off Homeric battles. And after all, what do we know? It does not do to be too sure that this, that, or the other hasn't happened and couldn't have happened.

A rather less noble faculty is the propensity of some to embroider and lie. The following chapters are peppered with barefaced fictions passed off as fact: ordinary soldiers who saw with their own eyes the visions at Mons or the crucified soldier at Ypres, despite being posted elsewhere at the critical time, and civilians who saw the Russian armies traversing England on trains, or spies disembarking from Zeppelins on Hackney Marshes. These accounts are characterised by self-aggrandizement, and a desire to be seen as part of a privileged minority in the know. Officers and gentlemen were no less prone to spreading Big Lies, however, as is clear from the pornographic atrocity fantasies of Major Corbett-Smith, Brigadier Morrison's vanishing corpses at Vimy Ridge, and almost anything written or said on the subject by Brigadier-General John Charteris, Haig's former Chief of Intelligence. Others may more charitably be said to have been confused or mistaken, or else were able to satisfy themselves that in the midst of a titanic struggle between good and evil, certain falsehoods were morally true (if not factually so), and therefore beneficial to the Allied cause.

Just as the creation of myths and falsehoods could be seen as fulfilling a legitimate war aim, so too could belief in their reality. Indeed to doubt or deny even the most fantastical story exposed a sceptic to the risk of being condemned as unpatriotic, and even traitorous. Some have characterized this susceptibility as 'hysterical hallucination' on the part of the feeble-minded, but given the pressures and complexities of wartime life this explanation is overly simplistic. Rather, for the average Briton in 1914, belief in the reality of an infestation of Hun spies, and the need to remain constantly vigilant against the alien menace, gave some small sense of contributing to the war effort.

Ultimately, however, belief in the irrational must for the most part elude rational explanation.

James Hayward
September 2001

CHAPTER ONE

Spy Mania

In December 1911, during the Kaiser's state visit to London, a senior German naval officer formed the habit of visiting a barber's shop situated at 402A Caledonian Road. The shop was run by a British subject, Karl Gustav Ernst, the son of a German surgical instrument manufacturer who had emigrated to England during the 1860s. Since this somewhat obscure establishment was hardly the kind of place which a high-ranking attaché might normally be expected to frequent, this activity aroused the suspicions of the newly formed British counter-intelligence service, then called MO5 and headed by Captain Vernon Kell.

Kell obtained a warrant from the Home Secretary to intercept all mail sent to and from 402A, and placed the shop under regular observation. These letters revealed that some 22 paid German spies located at Sheerness, Chatham, Portland and elsewhere were communicating with a German handler named Steinhauer (aka Madame Reimers), and as such the shop was revealed as a front for the entire German espionage network in Great Britain. In this way MO5 were able to identify every member of the nascent spy ring, and on the morning that war was declared, August 4th 1914, a series of raids were executed by the Special Branch. Ernst was arrested for breaches of the 1911 Official Secrets Act, while swoops elsewhere netted another 21 professional spies. A single man escaped via the port of Hull. The following day another 200 suspected German agents were rounded up under the auspices of the new Aliens

Restriction Order, among them several waiters and higher officials from a number of West End hotels and restaurants. After a two-day trial at the Old Bailey in November 1914, Ernst, described disparagingly as a hairdresser, was sentenced to seven years in prison. At a stroke the entire German espionage network in Great Britain had been neutralized, and a curtain cast over the country at the vital moment of mobilization. Although further agents were sent into the field by Germany during the war, the network never really recovered.

The first such operative to arrive after hostilities began, a naval reserve lieutenant named Carl Lody, proved to be an ill-trained amateur. His letters were immediately intercepted, and after a six-week tour that took in Edinburgh, London and Liverpool and during which he travelled in the guise of an American tourist, he was arrested in October at Killarney in Eire. Tried by a court martial held at the Middlesex Guildhall in Westminster at the end of the month, Lody offered no defence, and on November 6th 1914 went down in history as the first man in 150 years to be executed at the Tower of London. Lody's trial, to which the press were allowed access, was widely reported, and did much to fan the flames of an already fierce national obsession. Michael McDonagh of *The Times* recorded:

> The prisoner sat in the dock between two Grenadier Guards armed with rifles and fixed bayonets. He was a young man, dark-complexioned and clean-shaven. What was most prominent in his features was his nose, which was remarkably long. . . . At last this spy business has yielded something sensational and dramatic – and real. Hitherto we have had but the gibbering phantoms of the inventiveness and credulity of disordered minds.

The 'gibbering phantoms' and mental disorder to which McDonagh alluded was the rampant – yet largely irrational – spy mania, which had gripped the collective popular imagination across Europe even before the outbreak of hostilities. In Britain, fictional and dramatic works such as *The Battle of Dorking* by George Chesney (1871), *The Riddle of the Sands* by Erskine Childers (1903), *The Invasion of 1910* and *Spies of the Kaiser* by William Le Queux (1906 and 1909) and

When William Came by Saki (1914) had also done much to foster the myth that a veritable army of spies were at large across the country, diligently touring the east coast in motor cars, flashing signals to airships and submarines, and arranging secret landings by aeroplanes in South Wales. Across the Channel in France the trend was, if anything, stronger, where works such as *La Vermine du Monde* furnished faintly absurd accounts of the ubiquity and consummate cunning of the Hidden Hand.

During the first few days of the war, the spy scare in Britain was coloured largely by factual reports of the destruction of the espionage ring run by Karl Ernst. Between August 4th and 10th it was variously reported that in London police had seized a quantity of arms and ammunition from an address in Chancery Lane, and had discovered at the apartment of a waiter named Hammer a Winchester repeater rifle 'of the thumb trigger model', as well as maps and an atlas. In the City, members of the Stock Exchange were required to disclose the names and addresses of all foreign clerks, and enemy aliens were excluded from the banking business. At Dover a figure seen tampering with a telephone cable was fired on, but managed to escape. A small railway bridge at Guildford was reported as having been blown up on the 5th, and at Conway in Wales two men were arrested after a local claimed to have overheard them discussing a plot to blow up the steel bridge spanning the Menai Straits. Further north, the German Consul in Sunderland was arrested and remanded in Durham Gaol, while the following day all German males resident in the same town 'capable of bearing arms' were similarly detained, amounting to 60 in all. Like measures were taken in Manchester, Nottingham and Glasgow. In Liverpool, an Austrian cabinet maker named Berger was arrested and charged after being found on the premises of the 8th Battalion, the King's Liverpool Regiment, on suspicion of attempting to gain information likely to be of use to the enemy. More sinister still, at Edenbridge in Kent a troop train was fired upon, and a rifle bullet found in the woodwork of a carriage. The description of the suspect circulated by the local constabulary suggested 'spy' without actually saying so: 'tall and dark, with a sallow complexion and a dark moustache'.

The prevailing alarmist mood infected even the police and the armed services. Upon the outbreak of war, the Isle of Wight military warned that there were 'a number of spies' at large, and counselled the public against the risk of being shot should they be foolish enough to approach defences or military positions after dark. At Berkhamsted the Inns of Court Officer Training Corps (OTC) were called out to block the Great North Road, down which a German armoured car was said to be advancing towards London. On August 11th a Territorial was fatally wounded during a false alarm at Birkenhead, while a fortnight later a sentry from the Royal Field Artillery was shot dead by an unknown assailant while on guard at Holyrood Palace in Edinburgh. A distinctly ambiguous armed spy scare was noted in Essex near the port of Harwich at the beginning of September:

> The inhabitants of Mistley and neighbouring parishes were alarmed at 10.15 on Tuesday night by a quick succession of explosions. Some got out of bed and looked out from their windows, whilst others congregated at street corners discussing the situation, some thinking that German aeroplanes or airships were dropping bombs. It soon transpired that a spy was discovered in the act of approaching the Tendring Hundred Waterworks station at Mistley Street, which is close to the Harwich branch railway and Mistley station, flashing an electric light. The military sentries on duty challenged the man, and getting no answer fired volley after volley and chased him. The man eventually escaped through a wood in the vicinity, and none of the shots apparently stopped his progress.

At nearby Chelmsford, the location of the sensitive Marconi wireless works, a 'tragic happening' was recorded by a local vicar on November 5th:

> At the Marconi station there, one of the sentries was shot dead. It was presumed that this was done by German agents in a motor. Hasty telephones in all directions to the troops to close outlets

from Chelmsford. This brought troops in fiery haste from Broomfield to the ash tree at Waltham.

Some have suggested, however, that these stories of shootings were a deliberate invention, intended to keep troops on their toes. Another example of nervous Territorials is drawn from the memoirs of Sir Basil Thomson, who had been made head of CID at Scotland Yard in June of the previous year, and as such also controlled the Special Branch. On August 5th, Thomson records a visit to the War Office for a meeting with a senior intelligence officer, in order to obtain authority to evict a number of alien tenants from leased railway arches:

While I was talking to him it grew dark, and there was a sudden peal of thunder like an explosion. He said, quite gravely, 'A Zepp!' That was the state of mind we were all in. That same night my telephone became agitated; it reported the blowing up of a culvert near Aldershot and of a railway bridge in Kent. I had scarcely repeated the information to the proper authority when the bell rang again to tell me that both reports were the figments of some jumpy Reservist patrol.

At the same time the Yard announced that the effect of the new Aliens Restriction Order (ARO) was to place enemy aliens under 'certain disabilities' in respect of the possession of firearms, motor vehicles, petroleum, homing pigeons, wireless sets and sundry other articles. Aliens were also subjected to strict registration requirements, and barred from prohibited areas, chiefly coastal and military districts. At the same time the Defence of the Realm Act (DORA) made espionage a military offence triable by court-martial, under penalty of death.

Taken together, and read at face value, these various reports, rumours and measures gave the impression of constant and widespread espionage activity by desperate enemy agents. Michael McDonagh, a *Times* journalist, kept a valuable journal throughout this period, published in 1935 as *In London During the Great War*. On

August 11th McDonagh recorded the general tenor of the perceived spy peril:

> That jade Rumour has begun to flap her wings. London is said to be full of German spies. Popular resentment against German tradesmen, principally bakers, provision dealers, watchmakers, waiters and barbers, has developed in some instances into wrecking their shops. It is said that German purveyors of food are putting slow poison in their commodities. As for barbers, it is said you run the risk of having your throat cut by them instead of your hair.

So deep ran the fear of the alien peril that on August 9th the Home Secretary was obliged to issue a formal statement, promising that:

> The public can rest assured that the great majority of Germans remaining in this country are peaceful and innocent persons from whom no danger is to be feared.

Predictably, this appeal to reason fell on deaf ears. Between the 11th and the 18th it was reported that no less a figure than the Mayor of Deal had been arrested on suspicion of espionage, and that the cells at Felixstowe were filled to overflowing with men arrested as spies. At Aldershot a military picket claimed to have arrested two men caught cutting telephone wires, and at Fishguard a pair of 'well-dressed Germans' was detained after their bags were found to contain bombs and wire cutters. As a result of police activity in London, so it was said, enemy reservists and agents had hastily abandoned stockpiled arms, with the result that quantities of rifles and ammunition had been found 'in waste spaces and unoccupied houses' across the city. At Mile End a council worker was slightly injured after picking up a brass cylinder containing nitroglycerine. In all likelihood, these weapons had been dumped by their owners for fear of attracting at very least a punitive fine under the Aliens Restriction Order, and were hardly the actions of ruthless saboteurs.

The spy mania was particularly rife in garrison towns such as Colchester and Aldershot. In the latter it was widely rumoured in

September 1914 that a German had been caught at the waterworks with a quantity of poison concealed inside his shirt. The spy, it was said, had been the 'chief hairdresser' in Aldershot for 20 years. Writing to his brother in Canada, a local named Oliver gleefully reported that the man:

> Was put up against a wall and shot forthwith . . . As far as I can make out, some hundreds of spies have been shot at naval and military barracks since the opening of the war, though not a single one of the cases has been in the papers.

In the wake of such reports, anti-German paranoia blossomed quickly to manifest itself in a variety of activities. During the first few days of the war these were for the most part petty: German spa water, previously a favourite at fashionable tables, was spurned in favour of English water from Buxton. In theatrical circles it was seen as treason to use Leichner's greasepaint, previously regarded as the best money could buy. The *London Gazette* began to publish a steady stream of official notices of changes in the surnames of British citizens of German origin, and also of shops and companies. A number of firms also took out conspicuous press advertisements to reassure customers that their shareholders and workers were British through and through. Indeed the grocers Liptons were so nettled by unpatriotic smears instigated by their commercial rival Lyons that they threatened to utter a libel writ. On a different level of commerce, German prostitutes in Piccadilly became 'Belgian' overnight.

However, the spy mania soon took on a more violent hue. Famously, dachshund dogs (though not apparently Alsatians) were put to sleep or attacked in the streets, a persecution which endured so long that in the years following the war the bloodline had to be replenished with foreign stock. Before long this xenophobia resulted in outbreaks of serious violence. As early as August 9th anti-German disturbances broke out in Peterborough, resulting in a reading of the Riot Act. Two days later McDonagh observed in London:

All I could discover as I walked about town is that in the windows of German provision shops, such delicatessen as sauerkraut and liver-sausage are now labelled 'Good English Viands' and that Union Jacks are being flown over the doors . . . But these precautions did not save some of the shops in the East End from being plundered. The delicatessen was carried off and eaten, and no doubt it was enjoyed none the less because of its German origin.

On August 12th *The Times* was able to report that only two bakers and a grocer had been physically attacked in the capital, although this figure is probably an underestimate. Their largely sympathetic correspondent went on to state:

So far the evidence goes to show that the perpetrators of acts of violence have not been Englishmen, but the more lawless of the other foreign elements, between some of whom and the German residents feeling always runs high. At present the Germans themselves are for the most part keeping outwardly serene; but not a few are silently disposing of their businesses at any figure that they can get, and are preparing to disappear.

Reports of German atrocities against Belgian and French civilians began to circulate in earnest during the third week of the war. Like the imagined spy peril, reports of German 'frightfulness' across the Channel were frequently wildly exaggerated, but nonetheless played a part in fuelling xenophobia in Britain. On October 18th riots broke out in Deptford, where for three nights a mob of 5,000 roamed the streets looting German shops and restaurants, starting fires, and singing patriotic songs. Order was restored only by the intervention of 200 police officers and 350 men of the Army Service Corps. The riots triggered by the sinking of the *Lusitania* in May 1915, and the alleged crucifixion of a Canadian soldier at Ypres, were worse still. Outbreaks of mob violence were not confined to the capital, and in Keighley several pork butchers had their shops attacked and looted. According to one eyewitness the hostile crowd was mostly Irish, and drunk, and had been stirred into action by reports of German atrocities in Belgium.

After the initial spate of factual arrests and seizures in August, the spy mania took on an increasingly fantastical aspect as tall stories were further improved by word-of-mouth, or simply invented. The press also played an enthusiastic part in the myth-making, as this vitriolic comment from *The Times* of August 25th clearly demonstrates:

Many of the Germans still in London are unquestionably agents of the German government, however loose the tie may be. . . . They had in their possession arms, wireless telegraph apparatus, aeroplane equipment, motor-cars, carrier-pigeons, and other material which might be useful to the belligerent. The weapons seized by the police make an extensive armoury. They are more numerous than had been suspected. There are Mausers, rook rifles (strange weapons to be found in London suburbs), and pistols. Some of the rifles are of an old pattern and were obviously used in the Franco-German War of 1870 . . .

It has been remarked by the observant that German tradesmens' shops are frequently to be found in close proximity to vulnerable points in the chain of London's communications such as railway bridges . . . The German barber seems to have little time for sabotage. He is chiefly engaged in removing the 'Kaiser' moustaches of his compatriots. They cannot, however, part with the evidences of their nationality altogether, for the tell-tale hair of the Teuton will show the world that new Smith is but old Schmidt writ small.

Michael McDonagh records some of the wilder spy legends in circulation in Britain by the end of October, at the same time reflecting a degree of scepticism that was all too rare.

A large section of the public continue to suffer from the first bewildering shock of being at war. Their nerves are still jangling, and they are subject to hallucinations. They would seem to be enveloped in a mysterious darkness, haunted by goblins in the form of desperate German spies . . . The wildest stories are being circulated by these people of outrages committed by Germans in our midst. Attempts have been made to the destroy the permanent ways of railways and wreck trains! Signalmen in their boxes, and armed sentries at bridges, have been overpowered by bands of Germans who have arrived speedily on the scene and, their foul work done, as speedily vanished! Germans have been caught red-handed on the East Coast, signalling with lights to German submarines. Carrier pigeons have been found in German houses! More damnable still, bombs have been discovered in the trunks of German governesses in English country families! The fact that these things are not recorded in the newspapers does not prove them untrue – at least not to those subject to spy mania.

To this stock of rumour and legend McDonagh might have noted that spies had been busy causing 300 horses to stampede at the camp of the Staffordshire Yeomanry at Bishops Stortford, as well as organising hit-and-run attacks in assorted motor vehicles, and the belief that all 'Germhuns' employed by water boards and gas, electricity and tramway companies were sleepers patiently awaiting the call to sabotage essential utilities on the eve of invasion. Armed bands were raised, and only later brought under official control as the Volunteer Training Corps, a forerunner of the Home Guard a quarter century later. By the time McDonagh wrote the passage quoted above, the Home Office had issued a statement on September 4th intended to calm the panic and sporadic riots:

Articles and correspondence which have been printed in some of the newspapers show that there are symptoms of uneasiness and even alarm in regard to the presence in London and other parts of the country of large numbers of German and Austrian subjects, and stories have been freely circulated of alleged cases of espionage and outrage . . .

The military authorities and the Home Office had kept observation for a long time on the operations of such persons in all their ramifications, and a large number who were known to be, or suspected of being, engaged in espionage were, when war became inevitable, immediately arrested in different parts of the country. It is believed that the most active of the foreign agents were caught in this way.

Apart from breaches of the regulations, no actual case of outrage has been brought to the notice of the police or the military. A number of statements have appeared in the press, but when these have been investigated they have proved to be without foundation. For instance a few days ago there appeared in the press a circumstantial report of a midnight attack by two men on a signalman. As a result of enquiry it was found that the signalman was suffering from nervous breakdown and there was no truth in his story. There was no suggestion of any attempt to wreck a train.

There have been reports of attacks on police constables by armed motorcyclists, but in no case was the report substantiated. The stampedes of horses at a Yeomanry camp were attributed to malicious persons, but careful enquiries disclosed not even the slightest ground for suspicion. A few cases of aliens having failed to declare possession of a gun or revolver have been suitably dealt with under the Aliens Restriction Order, but the reports of the discovery of secret arsenals are untrue.

However, official denials of spy favourites such as the bludgeoned signalman and the murderous motorcyclist did little to dampen public interest, or credulity. For as the Commons were told in November, 9,000 Germans and Austrians were by then being held in detention camps, while 120,000 reported cases of suspicious activity had been investigated, and 6,000 properties searched. For many the figures spoke for themselves, so much so that during its first week of publication in 1915, the sensationalist book *German Spies in London* sold an equally impressive 40,000 copies. McDonagh again:

What about the Press Censorship? The Government deny that there is any foundation whatever for the rumours; but then the Government – these people argue – are not going to admit what everyone knows them to be – footlers, blind as bats to what is going on around them. Why, they have even failed to see that tennis courts in country houses occupied by the Germans were really gun platforms.

The myth of secret enemy gun platforms was one of the most widespread and enduring falsehoods prevalent on the Home Front. The rumour first entered into circulation after a war correspondent described how the Germans had utilized secret gun emplacements disguised as tennis courts during their bombardment of Mauberge. In the event of a German invasion of Britain, it was whispered, hidden artillery would be wheeled out, or raised from underground hides, to assist in the destruction of key points within range. The Reverend Andrew Clark, the parish vicar at Great Leighs near Chelmsford, recorded a local rumour from December 1914:

Miss Gold says that in Little Waltham the populace have discovered another German fort: 'Cranhams' was owned by Herr Wagner, who is now said to be an Austrian. Formerly some called him a Russian, others a Pole. The villagers say that at Cranhams, (a) there is a concrete floor for the emplacement of heavy guns of a fort which would command Chelmsford and the Marconi works there; and (b) there is a store of arms and ammunition.

A few tennis courts in London were inspected and probed, although none appear to have been dug up. Nonetheless, according to Basil Thomson:

Given a British householder with a concrete tennis court and pigeons about the house, and it was certain to be discovered that he had quite suddenly increased the scale of his expenditure, that heavy cases had been delivered at the house by night, that tapping had been overheard, mysterious lights seen in the windows, and that on the night of the sinking of the Lusitania he had given a dinner-party to naturalized Germans . . . For many weeks denunciations poured in at the rate of many hundreds a day.

Paved gardens, ornamental lakes and flat roofs also fell under suspicion, particularly where situated on high ground. In October 1914 the police raided a lithograph factory in Willesden, constructed from concrete with a floor and foundations built to an unusually robust specification. The factory was a single storey building and boasted an unbroken view over London to the Crystal Palace, as well as being situated close to a railway line. A crowd jeered as about 20 enemy aliens 'of military age' were escorted from the factory, it having been discovered that the firm had an office in Leipzig. According to the architect, the solid foundation was necessary in case it was decided to raise the building higher, although entirely rational explanations of this kind did little to allay a fear that fanned out across the country and even crossed the Atlantic to California. That same month one correspondent wrote to the *Daily Mail* to demand:

> Is it too much to ask that our kid gloved government will ascertain how many German owned factories have been built in this country which incidentally command Woolwich, Dover, Rosyth? A timely inspection might reveal many concrete structures.

One celebrated gun-platform report led to the issuing of libel writs against the *Evening News* and the *People*. The former paper had published an article suggesting that a concrete-bottomed lake in the Japanese garden of Ewell Castle, a house near Epsom, was capable of mounting five heavy guns to command the main railway line to London. The property was owned by Captain Clarence Wiener, a naturalized American born in Austria, who had commissioned the lake early in 1914. The paper detected further evidence that Wiener was a spy in the fact that he possessed a 80hp car equipped with a 500 candle-power acetylene searchlight. In July 1916 a local MP, Watson Rutherford, was induced to ask a question in the Commons about Ewell Castle, with the object of allaying suspicions. The bid failed, and ultimately Wiener sued for libel, even going so far as to instruct the celebrated barrister Edward Marshall Hall to clear his name. At trial, in April 1917, evidence was given that the concrete had been laid down by a landscape gardener to prevent the water from escaping from the lake. A local doctor also asserted that he had never known Wiener display any pro-German tendency. However, Wiener fought shy of answering potentially embarrassing questions relating to his private life, and was censured by the judge, Mr Justice Darling, for writing threatening letters to his former butler. The plaintiff scored a pyhrric victory: damages of just £50 and £25 respectively were awarded against each of the papers.

Another early spy scare involved homing pigeons, the possession of which by enemy aliens had been proscribed under the ARO. All pigeon lofts in the country were sealed up, and owners put to strict proof that they were the legitimate owners of the birds in their possession. On August 18th 1914 *The Times* reported the first of several prosecutions of pigeon fanciers, and by September, in order to secure convictions, the Crown was even calling in expert evidence on how far certain birds might be able to fly. Also in August another German 'hairdresser', named Schauber, received six months for possessing seven pigeons and a revolver, while one unfortunate foreigner actually found himself summonsed on the information of the wife of an ex-army officer, who gave sworn evidence that:

> On Tuesday afternoon she was on Primrose Hill when the prisoner passed by, and she noticed a pigeon on a level with his head, and about three yards in front of him, flying away with a little white paper under its wing.

For which outrage the accused was convicted, and sentenced to six months. At Maldon in Essex a local man fell under suspicion after a carrier pigeon landed on the roof of his house, causing an anxious crowd of several hundred to assemble. A police search of the house revealed nothing untoward, and after the bird's owner was traced it transpired that the creature was simply lost. By November the *Daily Mail* was reporting that carrier pigeons, all with nefarious intent, were being sent off in droves from neutral shipping.

Following the first Zeppelin raid on the British mainland, over Sheringham, Great Yarmouth and King's Lynn in January 1915, strict blackout precautions were imposed. Predictably, reports of mysterious night signalling rapidly increased in number and were boosted by each successive air raid. What appeared to be morse signals from a window in, say, Bayswater, were believed by some to be directed towards German submarines in the Channel or North Sea, despite the fact that these pinprick flashes could scarcely be seen from a window on the opposite side of the street. Thomson of the Yard offered a sceptical view:

> It was not safe to ignore any of these complaints, and all were investigated. In a few cases there were certainly intermittent flashes, but they proved to be caused by the flapping of a blind, the waving of branches across a window, persons passing across a room, and, in two instances, the quick movements of a girl's hair-brush in front of the light. The beacons were passages of light left unshrouded. The Lighting Order did much to allay this stage of the disease. Out of many thousand denunciations I have been unable to hear of a single case in which signals to the enemy were made by lights during the war.

Similarly, in Norfolk a vigilant Territorial officer posted near Dereham observed what he took to be suspicious signalling lights from the top of a nearby church tower. Assembling a party of men, the group advanced on the church with fixed bayonets and were about to open fire on several shadowy figures in the steeple when it was realised that their targets were troops from another company. Their comrades had seized the opportunity to carry out some unscheduled signalling practice. And as late as October 1917 the writer D.H. Lawrence was ordered by police to leave Cornwall following a raid on a dinner party at Bosigan Castle, at which – so locals alleged – signals had been flashed to a German submarine.

Even the First Lord at the Admiralty, Winston Churchill, fell prey to the mania, albeit while in drink. On September 17th 1914 Churchill visited the Grand Fleet, which was moored at Loch Ewe, a remote deepwater anchorage on the north-west coast of Scotland. After a long night in the wardroom of Admiral Jellicoe's flagship, the

Iron Duke, Churchill became convinced that the owner of a nearby mansion, a retired Tory MP named Arthur Bignold, was signalling to the enemy with the aid of a searchlight mounted on his roof. Undeterred, Churchill set about commandeering arms and ammunition from the *Iron Duke*'s armoury, and mustered a somewhat over-qualified landing party which included Rear-Admiral Sir Horace Hood, Commodores Keyes and Tyrwhitt and Vice-Admiral Henry Oliver, the then Director of Naval Intelligence. This brass-heavy group held Bignold and his butler at pistol point while a search of the house was conducted, although little was established beyond the fact that the searchlight was not in working order. Indeed, it is abundantly clear from private correspondence that Churchill and his wife Clementine were obsessed with phantom spies and saboteurs.

A close relative of the signalling mania was the belief that illicit wireless messages were passing to and from the enemy. The scare was given impetus following a pronouncement by an expert that an effective aerial array could be concealed in a chimney, and messages received on an iron bedstead. As with night signalling, reports of this kind often coincided with Zeppelin raids, for example that recorded by the Reverend Clark in September 1915:

Monday 27 September: Yesterday I heard a long story about Mr Seabrook of Broomfield. When the Zeppelin dropped bombs on Maldon, Seabrook was there with his car. When it passed over Witham and Broomfield on its way to London, Seabrook was there. On both occasions of its visiting Chelmsford, Seabrook was there. The report was that he was held up on occasion of the second air raid on Chelmsford, and his motor car was found to have a wireless-installation in it. Whereupon he was arrested. This evening there is a report in the village, purporting to have come from a 'military man in London' that Seabrook has been court-martialled and shot. Such reports, however, about detection and shooting of spies and secret agents have been common. Confirmation of any of them is lacking.

During the same month Clark recorded:

Friday 3 September: Mr Mitchell is manager of the Marconi Works at Chelmsford: says he is certain that there are three houses in Chelmsford in communication with the enemy's agents outside that town, partly by means of wireless, partly by flashing signals. They send their wireless when Marconi Works are busy sending messages so that their electrical discharges pass unperceived.

A popular play written by Lechmere Worral and Harold Terry, *The Man Who Stayed at Home*, discussed below, no doubt played a part a part in spreading the wireless spy myth far and wide, while according to Thomson:

At this period the disease attacked even naval and military officers and special constables. If a telegraphist was sent on a motor-cycle to examine and test the telegraph poles, another cyclist was certain to be sent by some authority in pursuit. On one occasion the authorities dispatched to the Eastern Counties a car equipped with a Marconi apparatus and two skilled operators to intercept any illicit messages that might be passing over the North Sea. They left London at noon; at 3 they were under lock and key in Essex. After an exchange of telegrams they were set free, but at 7pm they telegraphed from the police cells in another part of the county, imploring help. When again liberated they refused to move without the escort of a Territorial officer in uniform, but on the following morning the police of another county had got hold of them and telegraphed: 'Three German spies arrested with car and complete wireless installation, one in uniform of British officer.'

Thomson also investigated a spy rumour attached to the destruction of Zeppelin *SL11* above Cuffley in Hertfordshire in September 1916, amongst the wreckage of which was found a scrap of paper bearing the name and address of a Belgian woman living in London. After a lengthy investigation it transpired that the note had been dropped by one of the thousands of onlookers who flocked to the scene after the crash.

Predictably, Zeppelins gave rise to a rich crop of legend. In September 1914 a local rumour in Cumberland held that a German airship was operating from a clandestine base near Grasmere, and flew sorties over Westmorland by night. The story was only dispelled after a Royal Flying Corps pilot undertook several patrols above the Lake District in a Bleriot monoplane, and saw nothing but glorious scenery. Perhaps the most improbable Zeppelin story concerned the landing of a saboteur on Hackney Marshes in October 1916. According to Mr S.C. Thomas, while in the company of a young lady named Hilda Cavanagh on the Marshes near the River Lea on the evening of the 19th:

> Hearing a swishing, droning sound, we looked up and saw a Zeppelin right over our heads at the height of 100 feet. Orders were barked out, a clanking sound and from about 40 feet from the rear a light showed. A basket was lowered, hit the ground ten feet from us, toppled over and a tall man got out. He looked all around, saw us and came to us, and asked the way to Silvertown in perfect English. I told him to follow the Lea towing path till he came to Bow. He had either one eye or a patch and carried a long parcel wrapped in black canvas. The basket was wound up and the Zepp pointed its nose upwards and went away at a very fast speed. Meanwhile searchlights madly fanned the sky searching for it. I went to Hackney Police and told them, but was laughed at. If any other persons were on the Marshes then perhaps . . . they will verify my account of a German landing in London.

Mr Thomas's attractive memoir is somewhat undermined by the fact that no enemy air activity was monitored on the day in question, either by day or night. Elsewhere in London, the cataclysmic explosion at the Brunner Mond explosives factory at Silvertown on January 19th 1917, in which 69 people were killed, yielded a host of wild rumours. The officer in charge of the subsequent inquiry noted that 'persons of every class' believed that the explosion was an act of aggression or sabotage. One version held that the factory had been bombed by one of two invisible Zeppelins built by Germany, which generated their own gas as they moved. Another held that Sir Alfred Mond was a German, and that the factory was a nest of enemy agents. Others found significance in the fact that the explosion occurred on the Kaiser's birthday, and on the first day of Sir Alfred's annual holiday.

Another metropolitan rumour which surfaced in 1915 predicted some form of unspecified enemy outrage on the underground. The most common form of the story was told against the background of an English nurse having brought a wounded German officer back from death's door. On parting, the German revealed in a flush of gratitude that the nurse should 'beware of the Tubes' come April. Thomson expanded:

> As time wore on the date was shifted forward month by month, to September, when it died of expectation deferred. We took the trouble to trace this story from mouth to mouth until we reached the second mistress in a London Board School. She declared that she had heard it from the charwoman who cleaned the school, but that lady stoutly denied that she had ever told so ridiculous a story.

Judging from the dates, the story was probably a result of the first German poison gas attack at Ypres in April 1915. Sporadic poison scares broke out across the country at various times, the inhabitants of one village in Gloucestershire becoming convinced in the autumn of 1914 that villainous German spies had doctored the blackberries in local hedgerows. *Mayfair*, the journal published by Maundy Gregory, told of a spy who had been arrested in possession of enough typhus bacilli to incapacitate an army corps. Another spy was widely believed to be touring the country on a motorcycle, disguised as a scoutmaster, handing out poisoned sweets to sentries. By 1918, the myth had mutated so that enemy aircraft were dropping poisoned confectionery in an attempt to kill British children. This version was probably sparked by the discovery in Hull of boiled sweets containing arsenic, subsequently traced to a manufacturing fault at the factory.

It was also suggested that agony column advertisements were being used by spies to pass information back to Germany. Since refugees were known to communicate with friends and family abroad by this method there was nothing inherently ridiculous in the idea, and Thomson's team found it necessary to check the *bona fides* of some of the more cryptic messages in order to allay public alarm. But as he records, even this task fell prey to fantasists:

> Later in the war a gentleman who had acquired a considerable reputation as a code expert, and was himself the author of commercial codes, began to read into the advertisements messages from German submarines to their base, and vice versa. He did this with the aid of a Dutch-English dictionary on a principle of his own. . . . In most cases the movements he foretold failed to take place, but unfortunately, once by an accident, there did happen to be an air raid on the night foretold by him. We then inserted an advertisement of our own . . . and upon this down came our expert hot-foot with the information that six submarines were under orders to attack the defences at Dover that very night. When we explained that we were the authors, all he said was that, by some extraordinary coincidence, we had hit upon the German code, and that by inserting the advertisement we had betrayed a military secret. It required a committee to dispose of this delusion.

Another scare linked with advertising involved Maggi soup. During the German advance through Belgium in August 1914 a correspondent from a London newspaper floated an inexplicable story that the enamelled iron signs for certain brands of soup, meat extract and chocolate were being systematically removed by the invaders, and that various instructions and details of local resources were written in German on the reverse. As a result volunteer 'screwdriver parties' hastily banded together across London and removed a large quantity of signage for Maggi soup, but without discovering any secret Hun messages.

Amateur spy-hunting became a national pastime, much of it little more than snooping and score-settling. It seems that in rural areas the constabulary, and Special Constables in particular, were only too keen to follow up any rumour, no matter how unlikely. In urban centres the position was different, and the constant stream of reports and denunciations put some considerable strain on police resources. It is reported that at one stage some 400 people a day were being reported as spies to the police in London alone. Indeed, in the opinion of Major-General Sir Charles Callwell:

> During many months of acute national emergency, while the war was settling into its groove, there was no more zealous, no more persevering and no more ineffectual subject of the King than the Self Appointed Spy Catcher. You never know what ferocity means until you have been approached by a titled lady who has persuaded herself that she is on the track of a German spy.

While all enemy aliens quickly came to be viewed with (at best) grave suspicion, waiters and governesses were singled out for specific attention. The legend of the treacherous governess took several forms, the classic version being that on a given day the governess of a well-to-do family was noted as missing from the midday meal, and that when her trunks were opened a cache of bombs, explosives or firearms were found concealed beneath a false bottom. Naturally, everyone knew someone who knew the woman's employer. A similar story told of a German servant girl at Bearsden, near Glasgow, caught with a trunk full of plans and photographs. Foreign waiters without number were also denounced as spies, and stories were legion of those who had involuntarily betrayed their muster point come Der Tag, or clicked their heels, or cursed in their native tongue. The *Daily Mail* recommended that right-thinking diners should refuse to be served by German or Austrian waiters, and demand to see the passport of any that claimed to be Swiss. According to the *Spectator* for October 24th 1914:

> We can very well understand the Home Office deciding that the work of a waiter, since it lends itself with such peculiar ease to the work of espionage, should not in wartime be practised by enemy aliens . . . A rule against them would be one to which no sensible person could object.

Thomson describes how on one occasion a 'very staid' couple paid him a visit in order to denounce a waiter in one of the larger London hotels, and produced documentary evidence in the form of a menu with a rough sketch plan in pencil on the reverse. They believed it to be a plan of Kensington Gardens, with the Palace buildings roughly delineated by an oblong figure. It transpired that the waiter, a Swiss national, had simply prepared a plan of the tables in the dining room, and marked a cross against those he was charged to attend.

An oft-repeated tale told of a chance encounter between a German officer and a British friend, the given location often being Piccadilly, the Haymarket or the Army and Navy Stores. The officer either clicked his heels or involuntarily returned a salute, then realised his error and made good his escape in a passing taxi. Another common version described an English girl who came suddenly upon her fiancé, an officer in the Prussian Guards, who shook her hand, then cut her dead before jumping onto a passing omnibus. Other Germans adopted different guises. One apocryphal story told that a woman travelling on a tram to Brixton noticed four women dressed as nurses, sitting in couples opposite one another. One of the nurses tossed a book to her friend, who instead of separating her knees to catch it – as a woman might – drew them together in the fashion of a man. When the nurses got out at South Lambeth Road the observant woman wasted no time in alerting the police, and was said to have received a reward of £50. In Braintree in April 1916, another cross-dressing German spy was said to have been betrayed by virtue of his oversized feet.

Other tales hinted at similar Hunnish perversions. In a letter to *The Times* in September 1914, an ex-army officer pointed out that in the window of a curiosity shop he had seen for sale two army officer's commissions, one signed by King Edward, the other by Queen Victoria: 'this in a town where numbers of Germans reside, and where two spies have lately been arrested, one in female attire'. No less fantastical was a claim by a concerned London lady, Miss Nora Fane, who in August had submitted several letters to *The Times* on the subject of high-level espionage:

In consequence of her letters on 'Highly Placed Spies', Miss Nora Fane, a lady living in the West End, has received anonymous threatening letters from various Germans. One was a typewritten letter in which the writer said he hoped that when the German army arrived in London from Paris, which would soon be the case, her house would be one of the first to be burnt and that she would be stripped and thrashed in her own drawing room.

Stories of generous cash rewards for information received formed a distinct strand of the spy mania. On February 8th 1916 the Reverend Clark recorded in his diary a story told by Miss Gee of Felsted:

This afternoon she had a minutely-told 'perfectly true' story. It was rather vague: thought it was Waterloo Station, but was not sure. A train was going off, taking soldiers to the Front. It was in broad daylight. A lady stepped back, as people do under this circumstance. In so doing, she trod on an officer's toe. He (an officer, mind you!) swore softly, and swore in German. By sudden inspiration, she dashed to the barrier and told the porter in charge . . . The lady heard no more about it until three weeks afterwards, and then she had a cheque for £100 from the War Office. I said nothing about this story.

I have my doubts about whether War Office cheques for £100 fly about exactly in this way, although (no doubt) public money is poured forth like ditch-water. And also, the same fable, adapted to the latitude of St Andrews, had been entered by me in these notes on 2nd February . . . A St Andrews lady travelling to Newcastle was suspicious about a man in her carriage. Wired to York giving the name of the carriage – heard nothing till six months later she got a cheque for £100 from the War Office 'for information received.'

Artists and bohemians seem to have been particularly prone to being denounced as spies. One unfortunate artist and his wife living in a rural cottage in the west of England were constantly harassed and abused by locals, despite the fact that both were entirely British. Hostile locals took to visiting the cottage during the hours of darkness, to rattle the doors and windows and shout out threats. On one occasion bricks were thrown at the couple, and a constant supply of spurious accusations laid with the police. The only ground to this persecution appeared to be that the artist was fond of wearing a soft, flat, wide-brimmed hat, and that his wife wore a cloak of an unusual cut. The local schoolmistress was moved to comment: 'If he is not a spy, why does he wear a hat like that?'

Graham Greene records that a German master at Berkhamsted fell under suspicion after he was spotted loitering under a railway bridge, without a hat. The rationale is hard to fathom, but a similar pattern was repeated elsewhere. A clique of writers living under the Malvern Hills soon discovered that any sort of unusual accent or behaviour was likely to sow the seeds of suspicion in those of rustic mind. The American Robert Frost was thought to be a spy on account of his New Hampshire accent, and stones were thrown at his cottage. Wilfrid Gibson's cottage fell under suspicion after a Dutch poet came to stay, as did a party visiting Edward Thomas, who arrived late at night, and included a Russian boy from Bedales School. Near Stroud, meanwhile, the painter William Rothenstein was reported on account of his foreign accent, and steadfast refusal to change his surname to Rutherston, as his brothers had. When he was seen drawing a railway tunnel his neighbours leapt to predictable conclusions, and noted that his farmhouse dominated the valley. Because he had laid down concrete floors, predictable accusations regarding secret gun emplacements flew back and forth.

D.H. Lawrence was also suspected of treachery. A pacifist, and in any event unfit for military service, Lawrence moved from London to Cornwall with his wife Frieda. However, his presence in the West Country attracted unfavourable comment and suspicion, particularly in the wake of negative publicity attached to the seizure and burning of copies of *The Rainbow*. Frieda was a German, and a cousin of the fighter ace Manfred von Richthofen to boot; unwisely the couple adopted the perverse practice of singing *lieder*, a form of German folk song, to piano accompaniment on becoming aware of rumours they were spies. Locals suspected them of provisioning German submarine crews along the coast, and these suspicions were taken seriously by the police, who took to following the Lawrences on country walks and conducted a search of their remote cottage while they were away in London. In October 1917 the police raided a dinner party held by the composer Cecil Gray at Bosigan Castle, described above, following which the two men were charged with breaking blackout regulations. Gray was fined, but Lawrence was ordered to leave Cornwall within three days, to avoid living in any prohibited area, and to report to the police whenever he moved. Lawrence recorded his feelings on the train journey back to London as he sat 'feeling that he had been killed; perfectly still and pale, in a kind of after-death'.

On at least one occasion persecution of this kind led to tragedy. In the Suffolk village of Henham, near Beccles, a schoolmaster was suspected of being a German agent, apparently because some years earlier a German friend of his son had stayed at the family house. Although the teacher had been born in Devon and lived a blameless existence in Suffolk for thirty years, the rumours persisted until he was ordered by the police to leave the parish, on the basis that the presence of 'suspicious persons' in coastal areas could not be tolerated under DORA. The threat of expulsion weighed so heavily on his mind that the man took his own life shortly before he was due to leave. In the view of Lord Stradbroke, the main landowner in the area, the locals had, by spreading untruths, killed their victim just as surely as if 'they had drawn the knife across his throat with their cowardly fingers'. His innocence was posthumously established.

The military were not immune, as Thomson records in *Queer People*:

Near Woolwich a large house belonging to a naturalized foreigner attracted the attention of a non-commissioned officer, who began to fill the ears of his superiors with wonderful stories of lights, or signalling apparatus discovered in the grounds, and of chasing spies along railway tracks in the best American film manner, until even his general believed in him. Acting on my advice the owner wisely offered his house as a hospital, and the ghost was laid.

Sometimes the disease would attack public officials, who had to be handled sympathetically. One very worthy gentleman used to embarrass his colleagues by bringing in stories almost daily of suspicious persons who had been seen in every part of the country. All of them were German spies, and the local authorities would do nothing. In order to calm him they invented a mythical personage named 'von Burstorph', and whenever he brought them a fresh case they would say, 'So von Burstorph has got to Arran,' or to Carlisle, or wherever the locality might be. He was assured that the whole forces of the realm were on the heels of von Burstorph, and that when he was caught he would suffer the extreme penalty in the Tower. That sent him away quite happy since he knew that the authorities were doing something.

Perhaps the most ludicrous spy myths were the broadly conspiratorial type which held that numerous royals, peers, financiers and magnates had been imprisoned in the Tower of London on charges of treason, and even shot. Probably the first such report concerned the Crown Prince, Louis of Battenberg, who was Austrian by birth, but generally supposed to be of German origin. Mountbatten had been appointed First Sea Lord in 1912 after a distinguished career in the navy, but resigned in October 1914 following a spiteful campaign led by a London evening paper, the *Globe*, which hinted darkly that the navy was not playing its expected role in the war. According to Horatio Bottomley in *John Bull*:

> Blood is said to be thicker than water; and we doubt whether all the water in the North Sea would obliterate the ties between the Battenbergs and the Hohenzollerns when it comes to a life and death struggle between Germany and ourselves.

Mountbatten nevertheless managed to find some black humour in the fact that he was reported to have been shot at dawn, and no doubt took some comfort in being sworn to the Privy Council by the King. Famously, in 1917 the Royal Family would substitute the name Windsor for Saxe-Coburg.

An equally fantastical report from a newspaper in Pittsburgh in January 1916 held that the founder of the Scout movement, Sir Robert Baden-Powell, had faced a firing squad 'without a quiver' following a conviction for selling secrets to the enemy. By way of an epitaph, the report offered that England had 'put into his last sleep one of the bravest soldiers who ever headed her armies into foreign lands' – lines which, according to Baden-Powell's biographer, the Chief Scout considered might make the death penalty his lifetime's achievement. Contrary rumours also circulated that BP was engaged in secret service work in Germany throughout the war. In June 1917 rumours circulated that Admiral Sir John Jellicoe had been court-martialled and shot for losing the Battle of Jutland, and that his wife had also been executed as a spy. Being one of the last people to leave HMS *Hampshire*, the ship on which Lord Kitchener sailed fatefully for Russia in June 1916, his death was said to be traceable to her actions as a spy. Pioneer aviator Claude Graham-White was also falsely reported as shot, a press muddle possibly caused by his having troubled to try to clear the name of his friend Gustav Hamel, who stood accused of defecting to Germany before the outbreak of war. These delusions undoubtedly owed something to the fact that twelve *bona fide* German spies, Carl Lody included, were indeed held in the Tower prior to being executed there.

A related myth concerned supposed high-level imposters. One such story held that a distinguished German field-marshal, August von Mackensen, was actually the British war hero Sir Hector Macdonald ('Fighting Mac'), who had committed suicide in Paris to escape disgrace following a homosexual scandal. The tale ran that Macdonald had faked his own death in 1903 and entered German service in place of the real von Mackensen, who was terminally ill. Meanwhile Lord Haldane, the Lord Chancellor and Secretary for War, was persistently denounced as pro-German and unfit for office. Prior to the outbreak of war Haldane had vigorously promoted Anglo-German friendship, had once described Germany as his 'spiritual home', and was widely renowned as a student of German literature and philosophy. As a result, Haldane became the most widely reviled public figure in Britain, and in his autobiography records that:

Every kind of ridiculous legend about me was circulated. I had a German wife; I was the illegitimate brother of the Kaiser; I had been in secret correspondence with the German Government; I had been aware that they intended war and withheld this from my colleagues; I had delayed the dispatch and mobilization of the Expeditionary Force. All these and many other things were circulated . . . The Harmsworth Press systematically attacked me, and other newspapers besides. Anonymous letters poured in. One day, in response to an appeal in the *Daily Express*, there arrived at the House of Lords no less than 2,600 letters of protest against my supposed disloyalty to the interests of the nation.

It was also said of Haldane that he owned a dog named Kaiser, and that he employed a 'full-blooded German chauffeur' who regularly drove him to Olympia where he 'hob-nobbed with the German prisoners and brought them cigarettes'. The hate mail directed at Haldane was so prodigious that his maid was obliged to burn it by the sackful. By his own account he was heckled at public meetings, in constant danger of being assaulted in the street, and even of being shot. Although in May 1915 he was dropped from the government and entered the political wilderness, by the end of the year he was still being cursed so roundly across the nation that *The Times*' military correspondent, Colonel Charles Repington, remarked that one might as well 'try to stop Niagara with a toothbrush' as attempt to end a dinner-table tirade against the luckless Lord. But Haldane was not alone. Margot Asquith, the wife of the Prime Minister, was popularly supposed to harbour lesbian and pro-German sympathies, as well as a German maid, and was thus held in similar odium, while several ministers and MPs were also denounced as traitors.

The enduring spy mania inspired countless dramatic and literary works of varying quality. During the first two and a half years of the war no fewer than 50 plays concerning spies were submitted to the Lord Chancellor's office, all of which were produced, and during 1917 and 1918 a further 43 spy dramas were performed. One of the first was a popular play, *The Man Who Stayed at Home*, written by

Lechmere Worral and Harold Terry, and based squarely on scaremongering rumours. The piece was set in an East Coast boarding house kept by a woman whose first husband was a German general, and whose son was a spy at the Admiralty. The hero, a monocled fop, at one point accepts a white feather from his fiancée, which he puts into his pipe and smokes. He is able to risk doing so because, unbeknownst to his dearly beloved, he is busy breaking up a local spy ring. The play offered an abundance of cliché: there was a naturalized German governess and a Dutch waiter who kept pigeons, each with a map or message tied to its leg. Behind the fireplace lurked a secret wireless set, while a U-boat skulked offshore, awaiting the requisite signal. The play spawned a number of imitators. *In Time of War* offered a German princess-spy, who passed herself off as a nurse while adding poison to the hospital water filters. Even as late as October 1918 yet another melodrama set on the East Coast, *The Female Hun*, climaxed with a British general shooting dead his treacherous wife, less than half an hour after his butler had been shot as a spy.

The writer John Buchan took full advantage of the spy mania, and found a huge audience for his celebrated trilogy of Richard Hannay adventures: *The Thirty-Nine Steps*, *Greenmantle* and *Mr Standfast*. The first of these appeared in 1915, and swiftly elevated Buchan to the front rank of British novelists, although by day Buchan was variously employed as a journalist and propaganda writer. The book's central and complicated chase sequence offered a vivid image of Scottish glens bristling with enemy agents, while the rest is a potent cocktail of derring-do and high intrigue. The central premise on which the trilogy is based is given early in *The Thirty-Nine Steps*: 'Away behind all the Governments and the armies there was a big subterranean movement going on, engineered by very dangerous people.' At the centre of the web is a sinister master spy who has to be outwitted by Hannay, the heroic colonial adventurer. In *Mr Standfast*, published in 1918, Hannay is ordered to infiltrate a cell of pacifists in the fictional town of Biggleswick, where treason is afoot, and proceeds to 'sink down deep into the life of the half-baked'. The books were skilfully written, and reinforced the popular myth of the ubiquity and cunning of German espionage networks – ruthless, exploitative, and endlessly wicked.

Arthur Conan Doyle also exploited the spy scare to bring Sherlock Holmes out of retirement for the second and last time. The short story *His Last Bow* was first published in the *Strand Magazine* and *Collier's* in September 1917, and was originally subtitled 'the war service of Sherlock Holmes'. The story itself is set at the beginning of August 1914 and concerns Von Bork, the chief German spymaster in Britain. On the eve of war Von Bork prepares to return to Germany with a rich haul of stolen documents, while awaiting the arrival of his chief informant, Altamont, who has gained possession of the key to the Royal Navy's signal codes. When Altamont appears, however, he overpowers the German, ties him up, and is revealed as Sherlock Holmes. It transpires that Holmes has also netted all of Von Bork's agents, and ensured that the information previously sent back to Berlin is entirely false. In the epilogue, supplied by the great detective himself, Holmes reveals that he was at first extremely reluctant to return to detection, and had been persuaded to don his deerstalker once more only after a personal intervention by the Prime Minister. Largely because of its overtly propagandistic intent, the book lacks the brilliance of its classic forebears, but proved popular enough in its day.

As the war progressed, the essentially naive spy mania of 1914 hardened into a more pernicious (if no more sophisticated) belief in the existence of a so-called Hidden Hand, involving a network of highly placed establishment figures bent on undermining the Allied war effort. This early form of the conspiracy theory is examined more thoroughly in Chapter Seven, but now a series of entirely harmless myths, which emerged during the first twelve months of the conflict, will be considered – the Russians in England, and the Angel of Mons.

CHAPTER TWO

The Russians in England

During the first few chaotic weeks of war, even the rampant spy mania was eclipsed by a widespread belief that thousands of Russian troops had landed in Scotland, and were passing through Britain on their way to the Western Front.

The story first entered into circulation during the last week in August, and spread with astonishing speed as eyewitness reports were received from every corner of the country. From the outset the press treated the story with a degree of caution, and so the rumour was spread almost exclusively by word of mouth. The Russians were observed landing at Aberdeen, Leith and Glasgow; they were fed at York, Crewe and Colchester; they were observed smoking cigars in closed carriages and stamping snow from their boots on station platforms. The supposed fount of information was invariably an anonymous railway porter. At Carlisle and Berwick-on-Tweed the Russian troops called hoarsely for vodka, and at Durham even managed to jam a penny-in-the-slot machine with a rouble. Four Russian soldiers were billeted with a lady at Crewe, who described the difficulty of cooking for Slavonic appetites. Rifles and lances were spotted in guards' vans, and waiting transports spotted at Folkestone, destined for Le Havre. The number was variously estimated at between 80,000 and 'little short of a million'. It was commonly believed that the Russians were bound for the Western Front, although some offered that their allotted task was to seize the Kiel Canal. It was even suggested, less kindly, that the Russians would throw in their lot with the Hun once they had crossed the Channel.

Successive variations on the basic legend, and the manner in which such stories were usually circulated, were recorded by the Reverend Andrew Clark, the rector of the village of Great Leighs in Essex:

Friday 28 August: Report current in Braintree – that a Russian force has been brought to Yorkshire and landed there; and that the East Coast trains have been commandeered to transport them rapidly south en route for the French theatre of war.

Sunday 30 August: On my way to church . . . Miss Lucy Tritton met me, jumped off her bicycle and told me that her father had heard from someone in the 'Home' office (she said) that a large Russian force from Archangel had landed in Scotland and was being speeded south by rail to take its place in the theatre of war in Belgium. I mentioned the report of Saturday's evening paper, that a train-load of 200 Russians escaped from Germany into Switzerland and France, had reached England. But Miss Tritton was positive that her information was authentic and correct.

Wednesday 2 September: Dr Young of Braintree told Miss Mildred Clark that on Sunday the Russian troops were fed in Colchester . . .

Thursday 3 September: Letter from Oxford from my aunt . . . 'It was said last Friday that 80,000 Russians passed through here, No-one was allowed to see them. But for several days, only one passenger train was running, and the railway would not send luggage in advance.'

Monday 7 September: Montague Edwards Hughes-Hughes, JP, of Leez Priory told me that an old servant of his had written that from her bedroom window she had watched train after train for hours, passing by night to Bristol. There were no lights in the carriages, but by the light of the cigars and cigarettes they were smoking, the black beards of the Russians could be seen.

In Perthshire, on hearing news that the Russians were passing through Scotland on their way to Belgium, Lady Olave Baden-Powell hastened to the nearest railway station to watch them pass through. Two days later she noted: 'Russian rumour now denied by General Ewart, who commands Scotland and ought to know.' In the same county one clearly deluded landowner boasted that no fewer than 125,000 Cossacks had crossed his estates. A newspaper in Cardiff quoted a marine engineer as vouching that he had sailed with the Russians from Archangel, and had been in the 193rd trainload to pass through York. A correspondent told the *Daily Mail* how more than a million Russians has passed through Stroud in a single night. Sir George Young was converted to belief in the tale by no less a person than Sir Courtenay Ilbert, clerk to the House of Commons, who found the many circumstantial accounts too persuasive to reject.

Yet another clutch of Russian rumours was recorded by Vera Brittain, whose diary formed the basis of her celebrated memoir *Testament of Youth*. Entries in early September record:

> Only that day I had heard from my dentist that a hundred thousand Russians had landed in England; 'a whole trainful of them,' I reported, 'is said to have passed through Stoke, so that is why the Staffordshire people are so wise.' But when I returned to Buxton I learnt that a similar contingent had been seen in Manchester, and for a few days the astonishing ubiquitousness of the invisible Russians formed a topic of absorbing interest at every tea-table throughout the country. By the time, however, that we started believing in Russians, England had become almost accustomed to the War.

Two decades later, the writer and journalist Arthur Machen offered an interesting parallel with his own legend of bowmen and angels at Mons:

> Some people may remember that England had an earlier source of comfort and consolation. I should say assurance, for I think it was almost in the first days of the war . . . that everybody was talking of 'the Russians.' '300,000 Rooshians,' as Jos Sedley

assured his sister, Amelia, were coming to our assistance. Their trains had been observed passing with drawn blinds, through Ealing, Moreton-on-the-Marsh, Rugby Junction – through any station and every station. There were myriad on myriads of them – and your friends got extremely cross if you hinted a doubt.

But the Russian hosts faded gently away, and the British army was left to fight its own battles at Ypres and elsewhere. And the Bowmen, who had turned into Angels, took the place of the forces of the Czar. Great numbers of people made up their minds that the story was true from beginning to end.

News of the Russians was spread by some who should have known better. Lord Wester Wemyss, then the Rear-Admiral commanding the Channel-based 12th Cruiser Squadron, recorded the following in his diary:

In letters from various friends I had heard many rumours of the presence of vast hordes of Russian troops in England on their way to the battlefields of France, but I could not bring myself to believe in the story. If indeed they were being embarked at Archangel, why not disembark them at Brest? But I received on September 3rd a letter from a very old friend, Commander Gerald Digby, who had retired many years ago but was now working at the Admiralty, telling me as a fact that 80,000 Russian troops were embarking at Southampton, truly a marvel.

One can only guess at the reasons why so 'stolid' a man as Commander Digby succumbed to such fevered enthusiasm, unless the Admiralty were deliberately spreading the rumour to bolster morale. The point about Brest is well made, and in the main the British press held the story at arm's length. Of the nationals, only the *Daily Mail* and *Evening News* published articles, which were respectively satirical and sceptical. The myth in its various forms was also gently derided by Michael McDonagh of *The Times*, who recorded on September 8th that:

There is being circulated everywhere a story that an immense force of Russian soldiers – little short of a million, it is said – have passed, or are still passing, through England on their way to France. They are being brought from Archangel – just in time before that port was closed by ice – landed at Leith, and carried at night in hundreds of trains straight to ports on the south coast. This great news is vouched by people likely to be well informed, but is being kept secret by the authorities – not a word about it is allowed in the newspapers – until all the Russians have arrived at the Western Front. It is said in confirmation that belated wayfarers at railway stations throughout the country saw long train after long train running through with blinds down, but still allowing glimpses of carriages packed with fierce-looking bearded fellows in fur hats.

What a surprise in store for the Germans when they find themselves faced on the west with hordes of Russians, while other hordes are pressing on them from the east.

Lord Bertie, the British Ambassador to France, noted the rumour in Paris on the same date:

Many people here will have it that 50,000 Russians have landed in England, en route for France; they do not say how they got to England! A Regent of the Bank of France was quoted to me as a good authority; my answer was that there are foolish Regents . . . Bob Vyner saw the Russians at Victoria Station! There is hardly anything that people will not believe or invent.

Since the rumour had a measure of military and propaganda value, at first the Press Bureau took no steps to deny it. Indeed when a telegram from Rome on September 9th appeared to give official confirmation of the presence of 250,000 Russian troops in France, the response given by the Bureau was suitably ambiguous: there could be no confirmation of the statements contained in the message, yet no objection to them being published. As a result the papers became more open in reporting the story, for example the *Daily News* for September 9th published the following:

The official sanction to the publication of the above (the telegram from Rome) removes the newspaper reserve with regard to the rumours which for the last fortnight have coursed with such astonishing persistency through the length and breadth of England. Whatever be the unvarnished truth about the Russian forces in the West, so extraordinary has been the ubiquity of the rumours in question, that they are almost more amazing if they are false than if they are true. Either a baseless rumour had obtained a currency and a credence perhaps unprecedented in history, or, incredible as it may appear, it is a fact that Russian troops, whatever the number may be, have been disembarked and passed through this country, while not one man in ten thousand was able to say with certainty whether their very existence was not a myth.

Five days later, on September 14th, the same paper displayed less caution when running a curious dispatch filed by P.J. Philip, its special correspondent in France. According to the *News*, his report served to prove 'the correctness of the general impression that Russian troops have been moved through England', although precisely who or what Philip saw with his own eyes remains unclear.

Tonight, in an evening paper, I find the statement 'de bonne source' that the German Army in Belgium has been cut . . . by the Belgian Army reinforced by Russian troops. The last phrase unseals my pen. For two days I have been on a long trek looking for the Russians, and now I have found them – where and how it would not be discreet to tell, but the published statement that they are here is sufficient, and of my own knowledge I can answer for their presence.

That same day, September 14th, and with the Battle of the Marne now won, the story was firmly denied by the Press Bureau, which stated officially that:

There is no truth whatever in the rumours that Russian soldiers have either landed in or passed through Great Britain on their way to France or Belgium. The statement that Russian troops are now on Belgian or French soil may also be discredited.

The next day the *Evening News* met this bulletin with a compendium of typical reports:

All roads lead to Rome, and the railroad from Archangel led everywhere. The Cossacks were seen – though the blinds were always down – at Peckham, at Chichester, at York, at Bristol, at Ealing, at Darlington, on Ludgate Hill Bridge, at Evesham, at Peterborough. A grey cloud of fierce, whiskered men went rolling down to Cheltenham, at Euston their passing closed the station for 36 hours; at Rugby they drank great draughts of coffee. In the East End children playing by the railway embankment were gladdened with showers of Russian money thrown to them from a passing train. Cossacks swarmed at Southampton, and a London milkman, clattering his cans to salute the dawn, saw the myriads of the north march past him in the silent, awful streets . . .

Of course, there was always this suspicious circumstance; you never met a man who had seen the Russians. You met a man who knew a man who had seen the Russians; and this should have aroused our suspicions.

Naturally enough, not everyone was prepared to accept that the 'fierce-looking fellows' sporting beards, cigars and fur hats were a fiction, as McDonagh noted in his journal on September 15th:

London is depressed today. The flower of our fondest hope has been suddenly blighted. The Press Bureau has issued an absolute denial of the rumour so widely credited a few days ago that an immense force of Russians had reached the Western Front through this country. Like everybody else. I kept the ball a-rolling, and the only excuse that can be offered is that it was a case of the wish being father to the thought. Indeed, looking back on the rumour now, the wonder is how it ever came to be believed in. Why, it not only invited suspicion but shouted for it. The story of railway

porters at Edinburgh having had to sweep the snow out of the
carriages of the trains conveying the Russians ought to have been
sufficient to damn the rumour.

Still, there are people so happily constituted that their faith in
the story is strengthened rather than shaken by the official denial.
'Believe you me,' they say with a delightful air of confidence, 'the
contradiction is meant to deceive the Germans. The Russian Army
is on the Western Front all right.'

Conspiratorial notions of a double bluff meant that the story
remained current until well into October, as the Reverend Clark
recorded:

Saturday 3 October: Popular belief in the passage of the Russians –
Archangel: Scotland ports: English railways: Cardiff and Bristol –
continues. The latest explanation of absence of news of them is
that their guns went down in the wreck of the 'Oceanic' off the
Scotch coast. They cannot get to work till fresh artillery is got for
them from Archangel.

Commenting on the myth in his memoir *Queer People*, Scotland Yard
CID Chief Basil Thomson observed:

There was nothing to be done but let the delusion burn itself out. I
have often wondered since whether some self-effacing patriot did not
circulate this story in order to put heart into his fellow-countrymen
at a time when depression would have been the most disastrous.

According to the account by Brigadier-General John Charteris, the
rumour also entered into wide circulation among troops at the front.
Charteris served as chief intelligence officer at GHQ until December
1917, and in 1931 published his wartime journal. In mid-
September 1914 Charteris recorded of one of his fellow officers:

M is full of stories of Russians passing through London; says his
sister saw them, and when I said I didn't believe it, retorted, 'Do

you mean to say my sister is a liar!' So that ended that discussion. I asked at GHQ about the Russians, and was told, of course, that it was rubbish. They could not get there and would have nowhere to go, if they did. But a lot of men here have got hold of the idea – all from home letters.

On November 18th the story was denied in Parliament by the Under-Secretary of State for War, Harold Tennant, in response to a question from a back-bench MP

Tennant: I am uncertain whether it will gratify or displease my honourable friend to learn that no Russian troops have been conveyed through Great Britain to the Western area of the European War.

The origin of the myth remained inscrutable, even to those who searched diligently at the time. A variety of explanations have been offered over the years, some of them more credible than others. According to Charteris, in February 1915:

The Russians in England (whom poor M's sister saw!) were undoubtedly the Territorial units moving through Great Britain on their way to ports of embarkation for the East. One youth here adds the embellishment that at a wayside station one bearded warrior, asked where he came from, said truthfully enough, Ross-shire, which sounded like Russia. Even without this embellishment, the explanation is adequate. We shall have may more such rumours before the war ends. A wise scepticism seems called for with regard to all unlikely rumours. Intelligence work teaches scepticism, if it teaches nothing else.

The Ross-shire version, also endorsed by Basil Thomson in 1922, was fleshed out by Lord Lovat in 1978. According to Lovat, the event which triggered the tale was the transfer by rail of the Highland Mounted Brigade (or Lovat Scouts) from Blairgowrie to Huntingdon in August 1914:

This started the rumour that a force of Russians had landed in the north of Scotland, and were on their way south. The fantastic story, which spread like wildfire, had some foundation, for it fitted in remarkably well with the movements of the Highland Brigade. More than a dozen troop trains had passed through Newcastle and York, travelling in succession during the hours of darkness. Many of the men on board were reported to speak a foreign language, wear curious headgear, and be uncommunicative and shy in manner. When asked from whence they came by benevolent ladies staffing a canteen on York platform, they could only murmur, 'Roscha' (Ross-shire). Those who have witnessed the hysteria of non-combatants in big cities will not be surprised that witnesses were soon prepared to swear that the strangers had snow on their boots, while others, even better informed, had learned from high officials the exact numbers in the Russian Expeditionary Force. Those who disbelieved such bunkum were suspected of being pro-German.

Various other explanations were offered at the time. One held that a food wholesaler in London had received a telegram announcing that 200,000 'Russians' were being despatched via Archangel, with reference to eggs rather than soldiers. Interestingly, MI5 files declassified in 1997 reveal 'eggs' to have been the codeword for troops used by prewar German spies. Another explanation told of an excited French officer with an imperfect grasp of English who went about near the front, demanding 'Where are ze rations?' From Paris, Lord Bertie offered that a ship had been due to leave Archangel for Britain with gold worth £8 million, and a number of British warships detailed to escort it, a precaution which might have aroused suspicion. It is also said that a few Russian officers had appeared in Scotland to take up staff positions and purchase munitions, but ultimately the unfamiliar garb and accent of the Lovat Scouts may be the most credible explanation. If so, as Liddell Hart noted, a statue in Whitehall to the Unknown Railway Porter may be long overdue.

Two curious sidelights are worthy of mention. In his definitive study *Falsehood in Wartime*, Arthur Ponsonby records that General

Sukhomlinoff, the Russian Minister of War, stated in his memoirs that the British Ambassador to Russia, Sir George Buchanan, actually went so far as to request the despatch of 'a complete Russian army corps' to Britain, and that British transports were to be brought to Archangel to give effect to the proposal. The Russian general staff, he adds, came to the conclusion that Buchanan had lost his reason. In his lengthy account, *The World Crisis*, published in 1923, Winston Churchill offered, in similar vein, that on August 28th he had written to Lord Kitchener to propose that 'a couple of Russian Corps d'Armée' be transported from Archangel to Ostend to 'strike at the German communications in a very effective manner', although the idea did not proceed.

Still more curiously, some sources hold that the phantom Russian horde might actually have had some material effect on the conduct of the war. At the end of August, on the suggestion of Winston Churchill, 3,000 British troops from the Royal Marine Brigade were landed at Ostend to bolster the crumbling Belgian line. One of the officers attached to the Brigade was a colonel named George Aston, who later recalled:

The outstanding occurrences which were most helpful were the 'Russian troops rumour' (about mysterious Russians arriving in Scottish ports and travelling southward by night) and the news that the Belgian division, driven out of Namur, was embarking at Havre and coming round to Ostend. The Russian troops rumour, told me by the correspondent of *The Times*, was very useful. My marines were dressed in blue, with round caps and no peaks. They might easily be taken for Russians by German spies. Crowds of civilians were travelling through Ostend for the south, and spying was very easy. I hoisted my huge Union Jack in the railway station for them to report, and I took care that the Russian troops rumour was told as a strict secret to as many people as possible. That is the best way to make sure of wide publicity; but although I heard afterwards that the rumour was believed by vast numbers of people in England, I thought at the time that it was almost too much to hope for its belief by experts in the German General Staff.

Aston could not have known that Churchill had announced the arrival of the Royal Marine force at Ostend to the House of Commons on August 27th, and that photographs appeared in the press the following day – a fact of which enemy intelligence sources must have been aware. However, even if Germany was aware that at least some of the reinforcements on the Belgian coast were British troops, other sources hold that the fiction of Russians in the same vicinity greatly worried the enemy. Writing in 1930, Liddell Hart records that reports of a Russian force on the Belgian coast may have caused the Germans to withdraw precious reserves from the Battle of the Marne in the south:

> On September 5th, the day when the French troops were moving forward to strike at Kluck, Colonel Hentsch, the representative of the Supreme Command, came to the threatened army with this ominous and despairing warning: 'The news is bad. The VII and VI armies are blocked. The IV and V are meeting with strong resistance . . . The English are embarking fresh troops continuously on the Belgian coast. There are reports of a Russian expeditionary force in the same parts. A withdrawal is becoming inevitable.' We know from other sources that the 30,000 marines had grown in the German Command's imagination to 40,000 and that the Russians were said to be 80,000. Thus the German flank army was left to face its ordeal with the belief that their rear was seriously menaced.

In addition, the official British war history, edited by Brigadier-General J.E. Edmonds and published in 14 volumes between 1922 and 1949, attributes the following to an insider at the German High Command:

> At this time (August 30th) there was no lack of alarming reports at General Headquarters. Ostend and Antwerp took a prominent role in them. One day countless British troops were said to have landed at Ostend and to be marching on Antwerp; on another that there were to be great sorties from Antwerp. Even landings of Russian troops, 80,000 men, at Ostend were mentioned.

The rumour also appears to have been fed to the enemy by the luckless German spy Carl Lody (aka Charles Inglis), whose brief career and ultimate fate were described at the beginning of the preceding chapter. Basil Thomson, the Head of CID at Scotland Yard in 1914, records that prior to his arrest in Ireland on October 22nd, all Lody's letters and telegrams to his controller in neutral Sweden were intercepted with ease:

> He wrote all his letters both in English and German in ordinary ink, without any disguise. His information would have been of comparatively little value even if it had reached the Germans, which it did not. The only report that was allowed to go through was the famous story of the Russian troops passing through England.

The letter in question had been posted from Edinburgh on September 4th and was intercepted by MI5. Written in German, it read in English:

> Will you kindly communicate with Berlin at once by wire (code or whatever system at your disposal) and inform them that on September 3rd great masses of Russian soldiers have passed through Edinburgh on their way to London and France. Although it must be expected that Berlin has knowledge of these movements, which probably took its start at Archangel, it may be well to forward this information. It is estimated that 60,000 men have passed, number which seems greatly exaggerated. I went to the depot [station] and noticed trains passing through at high speed, blinds down. The landing in Scotland took place at Aberdeen. Yours truly, Charles.

At his trial in October, Lody explained how he came by this information:

> In Edinburgh everybody was speaking about it. I heard it in the boarding-house and I heard it in the barber's shop. If I may say so

I heard it in the store where I bought my shirt; he was absolutely sure. He said he had got it from a friend and he had got his – well, from his intimate friend at the North British Depot, the station – and he says that he walked up to them that particular Sunday and I said, 'Well now you tell me about those Russians', something like that. Well I took the matter rather serious. I took it for granted one night, and I said in the boarding-house – I am not sure whether Mrs Brown will remember – we were chatting as usual and talking about the war and other matters, and I met Mr Brown. 'Well,' I said. 'It sounds so ridiculous that Russia should pass here and you do not hear anything in the papers: you do not hear in France?' He said, 'It is an absolute fact – there are 102 trains passed through it: I know it is an absolute fact they have passed through Edinburgh.' I knew it as rumours.

The only detail Lody missed was the presence of snow on their boots. But while it is possible that this scrap of disinformation reached the German High Command, it must necessarily have done so some time after the alarms recorded by Edmonds and Liddell Hart. Indeed in his 1969 study, *British Secret Service*, author Richard Deacon extends supposition regarding Lody and the Russians too far. For according to Deacon:

> Despite all his failures and blunders Lody, ironically enough, was taken more seriously by the Germans on the subject of his most foolish report, the arrival of the Russians. On the strength of this news received from Sweden the Germans detached two divisions to guard the Belgian coast against the possible invasion by the Russians. The loss of these two divisions from the main Western Front probably cost the Germans the vital Battle of the Marne.
>
> Officially the use the Secret Service made of the porter's story about the Russians has been denied. It was denied for a very good reason: intelligence services have long been aware that the Germans are apt to believe the most fantastic rumours, and to admit that this penchant had ever been exploited by the British could have done untold harm.

While it is undoubtedly true that so-called 'black' propaganda should be unavowable in order to be effective, whether the legend of the Russians in England paved the way for the French victory on the Marne in September must remain a moot point.

CHAPTER THREE

Mysterious Visions and Clouds

In August 1914 the Imperial German Army deployed one and a half million men grouped in seven armies against the Allies on the Western Front. Their task under the Schlieffen Plan was to defeat the opposing French armies as swiftly as possible, before turning east to conquer Russia. On August 3rd the Kaiser declared war on France, and on the following morning advance elements of his army crossed the border into neutral Belgium, thereafter proceeding to subdue the country in brutal fashion.

Attempts by the French to counter-attack in the south resulted in a series of costly reverses. The small British Expeditionary Force (BEF), consisting of just 100,000 men, grouped into one cavalry and four infantry divisions, arrived in France in the middle of August, and on the 21st began to concentrate around the small Belgian mining town of Mons. The BEF engaged the enemy for the first time along the Mons-Condé Canal on August 23rd, and inflicted a severe check on the Germans by virtue of sustained and accurate rifle fire. Meanwhile, to the east of the British line, the French were driven back into full retreat. Unable to secure either of its flanks, the BEF was also obliged to retire, much to the chagrin of the 'Old Contemptibles', who believed that they had won the day. Thus the BEF commenced its epic fighting retreat from Mons, slipping quietly away under cover of night. These men faced a gruelling ordeal of long, forced marches south on unmade or rough cobbled roads, with little food or rest, interspersed with fierce rearguard actions to hold off the relentless advance of the Germans, most notably at Le Cateau on the 26th. The exhausting strategic withdrawal continued until September 6th, when the Allied forces finally halted and dug in east of Paris. For many it had lasted fully twelve days and covered some 100 miles, with the BEF sustaining approximately 15,000 casualties en route. The Allied advance to the Marne began later in September, and was followed by the onset of trench warfare on the Aisne.

As Chief Intelligence Officer at GHQ, and a personal friend of General Sir Douglas Haig, Brigadier-General John Charteris was well-placed to comment on the dramatic events of August and September 1914. Indeed, Charteris recorded his observations in a series of detailed letters, which in 1931 were published in book form as *At GHQ*. An oft-quoted entry for September 5th 1914 records the following:

> Then there is the story of the 'Angels of Mons' going strong through the 2nd Corps, of how the angel of the Lord on the traditional white horse, and clad all in white with flaming sword, faced the advancing Germans at Mons and forbade their further progress. Men's nerves and imagination play weird pranks in these strenuous times. All the same the angel at Mons interests me. I cannot find out how the legend arose.

The answer, perhaps, was simple exhaustion. Of the retreat from Le Cateau on August 27th, Private Frank Richards of the Royal Welsh Fusiliers recalled:

> If any angels were seen on the Retirement . . . they were seen that night. March, march, for hour after hour, without a halt; we were now breaking into the fifth day of continuous marching with practically no sleep in between . . . Stevens said: 'There's a fine castle there, see?' pointing to one side of the road. But there was nothing there. Very nearly everyone was seeing things, we were all so dead beat.

A similar experience from the retreat, this time from a young officer, was related to Mabel Collins, author of *The Crucible* (1915):

I had the most amazing hallucinations marching at night, so I was fast asleep, I think. Everyone was reeling about the road and seeing things . . . I saw all sorts of things, enormous men walking towards me and lights and chairs and things in the road.

A more explicitly supernatural account, from an anonymous Lieutenant-Colonel also present at Le Cateau, was reported in the *Daily Mail*:

We came into action at dawn, and fought till dusk. We were heavily shelled by the German artillery during the day, and in common with the rest of the division had a bad time of it. Our division, however, retired in good order. We were on the march all night of the 26th, and on the 27th, with only about two hours' rest. The brigade to which I belonged was rearguard to the division, and during the 27th we were all absolutely worn out with fatigue – both bodily and mental fatigue. No doubt we also suffered to a certain extent from shock, but the retirement still continued in excellent order, and I feel sure that our mental faculties were still . . . in good working condition.

On the night of the 27th I was riding along in the column with two other officers. We had been talking and doing our best to keep from falling asleep on our horses. As we rode along I became conscious of the fact that, in the fields on both sides of the road along which we were marching, I could see a very large body of horsemen. These horsemen had the appearance of squadrons of cavalry, and they seemed to be riding across the fields and going in the same direction as we were going, and keeping level with us . . .

I did not say a word about it at first, but I watched them for about 20 minutes. The other two officers had stopped talking. At last one of them asked me if I saw anything in the fields. I told them what I had seen. The third officer then confessed that he too had been watching these horsemen for the last 20 minutes. So convinced were we that they were real cavalry that, at the next halt, one of the officers took a party of men out to reconnoitre, and found no-one there. The night grew darker, and we saw no more.

The same phenomenon was seen by many men in our column. Of course, we were all dog-tired and overtaxed, but it is an extraordinary thing that the same phenomenon should be witnessed by so many different people. I myself am absolutely convinced that I saw these horsemen, and I feel sure that they did not exist only in my imagination. I do not attempt to explain the mystery – I only state facts.

A Lance-Corporal Johnstone, late of the Royal Engineers, gave a broadly similar account in a letter to the *Evening News*. The events described appear to have taken place early in September:

We had almost reached the end of the retreat, and after marching a whole day and night with but one half-hour's rest in between, we found ourselves in the outskirts of Langy, near Paris, just at dawn, and as the day broke we saw in front of us large bodies of cavalry, all formed up into squadrons – fine, big men, on massive chargers. I remember turning to my chums in the ranks and saying: 'Thank God! We are not far off Paris now. Look at the French cavalry.' They, too, saw them quite plainly, but on getting closer, to our surprise the horsemen vanished and gave place to banks of white mist, with clumps of trees and bushes dimly showing through.

When I tell you that hardened soldiers who had been through many a campaign were marching quite mechanically along the road and babbling all sorts of nonsense in sheer delirium, you can well believe we were in a fit state to take a row of beanstalks for all the saints in the calendar.

As well as supernatural visions of angels, phantom castles and spectral formations of cavalry, the foregoing accounts all share another factor in common: all were published some considerable time after the events they purport to relate. Charteris published his memoir in 1931, Richards his in 1964, while the *Evening News* and *Daily Mail* stories appeared in August and September 1915 respectively. Furthermore, without exception, all were published long after the appearance of *The*

Bowmen, the celebrated short story by Arthur Machen first printed in the *Evening News* on September 29th 1914.

Arthur Machen, then aged 51, had worked as a staff writer at the paper since 1910, reporting chiefly on the arts and religion rather than current affairs. The son of an Anglican vicar, his true calling lay as a writer of gothic and fantastical fiction, a fascination which extended to his becoming a fringe member of the Hermetic Order of the Golden Dawn, a mystical society which also boasted Aleister Crowley and W.B. Yeats among its initiates. Although in September 1914 *The Bowmen* occupied just 17 column inches on the third page of a London evening paper, it immediately provoked a popular reaction out of all proportion to its size and intent. The rather quaint story was written by Machen to boost public morale, and as a personal response to the imagined horrors of a war just two months old. Two decades later he confirmed that the specific spur was a brace of highly alarming headlines which appeared on August 30th, a Sunday, when *The Times* told of 'Broken British Regiments Battling Against Odds' and the *Weekly Dispatch* revealed a 'German Tidal Wave – Our Soldiers Overwhelmed by Numbers.' The paragraphs beneath them were almost unique in the annals of First World War reporting, for they offered the public a truthful account of the military situation across the Channel, and Machen's shocked response was typical:

> I looked out of my window one Sunday morning towards the end of August 1914, and saw some newspaper bills in front of the little shop over the way, and saw that the night had come . . . I have forgotten the detail of the newspaper account of [the retreat]; but I remember it was a tale to make the heart sink, almost to deep despair. It told of the British army in full retreat, nay, in headlong, desperate retreat, on Paris . . . The correspondent rather pictured an army broken to fragments scattered abroad in confusion. It was hardly an army any more; it was a mob of shattered men . . . And I suppose that in the first place it was to comfort myself that I thought of the story of the Bowmen, and wrote it in the early days of September.

The Bowmen unfolds as follows: during a particularly fierce rearguard action against overwhelming odds, a British soldier suddenly remembers the dinner plates at a favoured vegetarian restaurant in London, decorated with the figure of St George and the motto *Adsit Anglis Sanctus Georgius*: 'may St George be a present help to the English'. In desperation the man utters this invocation aloud, and feels 'something between a shudder and an electric shock' pass through his body. At once the roar of battle dies away, and in its place he hears a tumult of voices calling on St George to 'grant us good deliverance' with 'a long bow and a strong bow'. As the soldier hears these voices he spies beyond the trench a 'long line of shapes, with a shining about . . . them', which resemble archers. With another shout the phantom bowmen let fly a cloud of arrows at the advancing Germans, who fall dead in their thousands. After the engagement the German General Staff, finding no wounds on the bodies of the dead, conclude that the British had used poison gas. However, the man 'who knew what nuts tasted like when they called themselves steak' knew also that St George had summoned Henry V's yew hedge of archers from Agincourt to save the beleaguered BEF.

The romantic imagery conjured by Machen was highly attractive, and so great became the popularity of *The Bowmen* that in August of the following year the story was reprinted as a short book, together with five other stories by Machen in similar vein. The author included a lengthy introduction, in which he claimed that his original story had been responsible for the 'snowball of rumour' that archers and angels had actually appeared over the field of battle. After expressing regret that 'queer complications' had grown up around his work of fiction, in which the word angels nowhere appeared, the author blamed religious bodies for exploiting what he considered an unremarkable story, and concluded that any sightings of spectral hosts were explicable as mere hallucinations. Machen had already given much the same response to interested psychical journals such as *Light* and the *Occult Review* in October 1914, and there the matter rested.

That is, until April 1915. Although Machen had agreed to *The Bowmen* being reprinted in a number of small parish magazines, seven months after it had first appeared in the *Evening News* the legend gained a second wind. Precisely what triggered this resurrection is unclear, given that an official War Office propaganda department did not yet exist. Nevertheless, during that month the magazine *Light* claimed to have been visited by an unnamed 'military officer', who stated that:

> Whether Mr Machen's story was pure invention or not, it was certainly stated in some quarters that a curious phenomenon had been witnessed by several officers and men in connection with the retreat from Mons. It took the form of a strange cloud interposed between the Germans and the British. Other wonders were heard or seen in connection with this cloud which, it seems, had the effect of protecting the British against the overwhelming hordes of the enemy.

At the same time the orthodox religious press now developed an equivalent fascination with the legend. Later in April a Roman Catholic newspaper called *The Universe* published an account from 'an accredited correspondent' based on a letter from an unnamed 'Catholic officer' at the front, which told of deliverance by phantom bowmen led by St George, and hordes of dead Germans – all of them unmarked. This account closely mirrors *The Bowmen*, and as such differed greatly from the next account to appear, courtesy of a Miss Marrable in the *All Saints (Clifton) Parish Magazine* for May 1915. Miss Marrable, the daughter of Canon Marrable, claimed acquaintance with two anonymous officers:

> Both of whom had themselves seen the angels who saved our left wing from the Germans when they came right upon them during the retreat from Mons . . . One of Miss M's friends, who was not a religious man, told her that he saw a troop of angels between us and the enemy. He has been a changed man ever since. The other man . . . and his company were retreating, they heard the German cavalry tearing after them . . . They therefore turned round and faced the enemy, expecting nothing but instant death, when to

their wonder they saw, between them and the enemy, a whole troop of angels. The German horses turned round terrified and regularly stampeded. The men tugged at their bridles, while the poor beasts tore away in every direction . . .

Although pressed to reveal her sources by various investigators, Miss Marrable declined to identify her informants more precisely. However, detailed analysis of the development of the various visions of 1914 reveals that the Marrable story marks an important turning point, in that it bears little resemblance to Machen's original story of Agincourt bowmen. In the subsequent angels legend there is no invocation of St George or foreknowledge of the words required, while the angels themselves have neither leader nor weapons, and no Germans are killed. Viewed in the round it has more in common with the reports of protective spectral cavalry, and the phenomenal cloud described by *Light*'s enigmatic 'military officer', than with the original bowmen fiction.

Bearing these substantial differences in mind, can Machen claim credit for originating the myth? In 1915 many thought not: in his pamphlet *On the Side of the Angels*, Harold Begbie emerged as a particularly vociferous critic, accusing Machen of 'amazing effrontery'. Begbie, in turn, was roundly lambasted by T.W.H. Crosland, in his own book *Find the Angels*. At least six more books and pamphlets supporting the reality of the angels appeared before the Armistice in 1918, as well as an Angel of Mons Waltz by Paul Paree. As late as 1966 A.J.P. Taylor described certain of the military reports (presumably Charteris) as 'more or less reliable', while in 1980, historian John Terraine also challenged Machen's ready assumption of sole responsibility, on the basis that Charteris had apparently written of angels as early as September 5th, and the fact that the anonymous Lieutenant-Colonel's letter to the *Daily Mail* had been published on September 14th 1914. But Terraine's source was wrong in dating the *Daily Mail* piece a full year before it actually appeared, and assumes that in 1931 Charteris published his wartime letters without editing or revision. That assumption must surely be questioned.

Ironically, the avowedly mystical Machen is probably correct, and the circumstances in which *The Bowmen* was published in the *Evening News* on September 29th may go some way towards explaining what subsequently transpired. Against a background of stringent War Office reporting restrictions and bland official communiqués, most papers had little option but to print personal accounts of battle by individual soldiers, the content of which readers were expected to accept at face value. The consequences were later highlighted by the war correspondent Philip Gibbs:

> Owing to the rigid refusal of the War Office, under Lord Kitchener's orders, to give any official credentials to correspondents, the British press, as hungry for news as the British public whose little professional army had disappeared behind a deathlike silence, printed any scrap of description, any glimmer of truth, and wild statement, rumour, fairy tale or deliberate lie, which reached them from France and Belgium; and it must be admitted that the liars had a great time.

Machen had been a leader writer on the paper for four years, but had not previously published fiction within its pages. Indeed, *The Bowmen* was not flagged as fiction when it first appeared, despite the fact that another fictional piece on a different page in the same edition was clearly headed 'Our Short Story'. To the general public, in a less media-literate age than our own, all of this may have tended to suggest that the bowmen described by Machen had actually appeared on the field, at a time when there was a pressing need in Britain to believe that the war had not been lost within the first eight weeks.

Thus uncorked, the genie refused to return to the bottle. By June of 1915 folkloric reports of angels, bowmen and protective clouds had become commonplace, and in the popular imagination came to represent the universal experience of the BEF on the long road from Mons. Tellingly, the contemporary sources were always second- or third-hand, and the witnesses, without exception, anonymous and untraceable. Several reports originated from Ireland and had a distinctly Catholic emphasis, while others took the form of quotes from sermons delivered by clergymen in churches and congregational halls, supposedly informed by letters from the Front. One vociferous believer was the Reverend Alexander Boddy, a vicar from Sunderland, who had served two months in the line in 1914 and publicized several anonymous tales of angels and spirit warriors. Another clergyman, who wrote to a religious periodical casting doubt on the truth of the story, was accused of revealing infirmity of faith. Inevitably, chinese whispers served to churn and embroider the legend still further, one example being that published in *Light* on May 8th 1915:

> General N, who also had been at Mons, [stated] that in that rearguard action there was one specially critical moment. The German cavalry was rapidly advancing, and very much outnumbered our forces. Suddenly, he saw a sort of luminous cloud, or light interpose itself between the Germans and our forces. In the cloud there seemed to be bright objects moving: he could not say if they were figures or not, but they were moving and bright. The moment the cloud appeared the German onslaught seemed to receive a check; the horses could be seen rearing and plunging, and they ceased to advance. He said it was his opinion that if that check, whatever its cause, had not come, the whole force would have been annihilated in 20 minutes.

The same source alleged that another (anonymous) officer had told that:

> After what I saw that day, nothing will make me doubt for one moment but that we shall win this war.

Clear inferences of divine sanction, deliverance and virtue can be seen in other variants of the angels legend. Previously a hard drinker, one Mons veteran, said to have seen the angels with his own eyes, afterwards became teetotal and a pillar of the community. A Nonconformist pastor preaching in Manchester, Dr R.F. Horton, offered that he had heard all those who had taken part in the retreat were changed men, and had felt a spiritual uplifting. Elsewhere, during the retreat around the dense Forest of Mormal, a detachment of Coldstream Guards were said to have become lost, and in grave danger of being overrun. An angel then appeared as a female figure in dim outline, tall and slim, and wearing a white flowing gown. The Guardsmen, it was said, followed the glowing figure across an open field to a sunken road, otherwise hidden from view, and were able to make good their escape. Naturally the incident does not appear in regimental histories or other primary sources, in common with every other version of the legend.

Whereas the likes of Canon Marrable's daughter and Harold Begbie were simply gullible, others were downright unscrupulous. Begbie found support in the dubious writings of Phyllis Campbell, by her own account a nurse in forward hospitals in France, whose booklet *Back of the Front* was published in late 1915, after being trailed in the *Occult Review*. The text is wholly propagandist, and dwells at length on the kind of discredited atrocity fantasies examined in Chapter Four. This familiar litany is followed by a highly embroidered version of the angels legend, now joined by Joan of Arc, St Michael and golden clouds. Exalted soldiers knew that they had seen St George, apparently, because they were 'familiar with his figure on the English sovereign, and had recognized it'. A brief example illustrates well the generally hysterical tone of Campbell's lurid reportage:

Poor Dix, when he came into hospital with only a bleeding gap where his mouth had been, and a splintered hand and arm, he ought to have been prostrate and unconscious, but he made no moan, his pain had vanished in contemplation of the wonderful things he had seen – saints and angels fighting on this common earth, with common mortal men, against one devilish foe to all humanity. A strange and dreadful thing, that the veil that hangs between us and the world of Immortality should be so rent and shrivelled by suffering and agony that human eyes can look on the angels and not be blinded. The cries of mothers and little children

– the suffering of crucified fathers and carbonized sons and brothers, the tortures of nuns and virgins, and violated wives and daughters, have all gone up in torment and dragged at the Ruler of the Universe for aid – and aid has come.

No more helpful was a report from the *Daily Mail* on August 24th 1915, in which it was stated that a Private Robert Cleaver of the Cheshire Regiment had signed an affidavit to the effect that he had been present at Mons, and had seen a vision of angels with his own eyes. The paper was rightly excited, since at no time had any firsthand testimony from an identifiable witness come to light. On September 2nd, however, the paper announced with regret that further enquiries had revealed that Private Cleaver's draft arrived in France only on September 6th 1914, from which readers could draw their own conclusions. A rigorous investigation conducted by the Society for Psychical Research in 1915 also reached a generally negative conclusion on the reality of the various visions:

Of first-hand testimony we have received none at all, and of testimony at second-hand we have none that would justify us in assuming the occurrence of any supernormal phenomenon.

Machen was again obliged to deny any factual element to his original short story in July 1916, following the publication of 'The First Battle of Ypres', a stirring patriotic verse by Margaret Woods. The poem told of 'enormous reserves' which appeared more than mortal, and which caused the Germans to retreat in a state of consternation. In the July 3rd edition of the *Evening News*, Machen observed:

Pending the production of real testimony, I am strongly inclined to think that this brave poem of brave warriors rising in dreadful array and gathering again to their ancient banners is the most worthy and valiant offspring of an unworthy father: *The Bowmen*.

So why did such an unlikely legend gain widespread credence? Begbie criticized what he saw as Machen's callousness in ignoring the depth of suffering caused by heavy BEF losses, and 'the intense eagerness for consolation' in England. The climate on the Home Front was clearly a highly suggestible one, with pantomime spies on every street corner and frosted Russian soldiers demanding vodka at every railway station. An almost total blackout on news reporting from France and Belgium until June 1915 meant that almost all wild rumour was likely to be believed, at least by a proportion of the population. Yet more than this, and in common with the atrocity stories from Belgium, the story had the ring of moral truth. The legend of heavenly intervention offered proof that God was on the side of the Allies, and that victory was certain. The capture of the first German prisoners in August had caused widespread indignation when it was discovered that the words 'Gott Mit Uns' were cast on their belt buckles. The Angel of Mons provided a perfect rebuttal.

General Charteris, in an entry for February 1915 mentioned in *At GHQ*, offers his own unlikely explanation for the genesis of the myth:

> I have been at some trouble to trace this rumour to its source. The best I can make of it is that some religiously minded man wrote home that the Germans halted at Mons, AS IF an Angel of the Lord had appeared in front of them. In due course the letter appeared in a Parish Magazine, which in time was sent out to some other men at the front. From them the story went back home with the 'as if' omitted, and at home it went the rounds in its expurgated form.

The angels made an obscure, if psychologically telling, swansong appearance above the Thames Estuary at Thurrock during the summer of 1917, as the latest costly Allied offensive on the Western Front, Third Ypres, bogged down in a sea of mud at Passchendaele. According to the *Grays and Tilbury Gazette* for August 18th:

> 'Have you seen the angels?' is the latest topic which is arousing interest in Grays. Although stories are varied, and, as usual,

conflicting, most circumstantial tales are going round regarding alleged angelic visitations seen from the beach on the evenings of Tuesday and Wednesday this week. It is not a case of the 'Angels of Mons' this time, for all the stories agree that those now seen are harbingers of Peace . . .

'All Argent Street was out after them,' said one speaker. 'They appeared over the Exmouth, two of them sitting on two rainbows with "Peace" in between. Then they faded away, leaving only the rainbow.' This was on Tuesday evening, when a rainbow did actually appear . . . Inquiries in Argent Street failed to elicit more definite confirmation, though it was clearly a similar version of the apparition that had been going the rounds. 'It was three angels, I was told,' said one speaker . . . 'They had roses wreathed in their hair,' added another story-teller, who had evidently heard a more detailed version . . .

In another version, coming from a relative of one said to have witnessed the apparition . . . the angels are generally seen about 9.30. According to her they are the 'Angels of Mons', but the description given is rather different from that of those legendary beings. These visitations are three angels seated and chained together, a long chain linking them up . . .

Everyone agreed that they were 'Peace Angels' and one prophesied that the 'Angels of Mons' were due to arrive next week. In fact, from all accounts the sea wall is likely to have an increase of traffic during the next few nights . . . Numerous mothers agreed that they had heard tales of 'angels' from their children, and generally expressed the opinion that probably the youngsters were getting a bit 'nervy' in the present times of stress, and hence the remarkable 'visions.' In all probability the tale had its origin somewhat in this way.

The following week this attractive story was given a new twist, the same paper reporting on the 25th:

A fresh version was given to a *Gazette* representative by a Globe Terrace resident. Speaking of the previous Tuesday evening, she said: 'I don't know about any angels, but I saw a wonderful cloud. We were out with my landlady and the children, and we were looking at the rainbow. Then I saw a white cloud a little distance away. It was shaped just like a woman.'

She continued: 'I don't know what it was, but it was just like a woman. It quite unnerved me. My husband is away in the army, and I thought it meant something over the water. I couldn't sleep for thinking of it. It was a wonderful thing. I've never seen a cloud like it before and don't want to again.'

The paper concluded that the so-called 'Riverside Apparitions' were caused either by the northern lights, or else a rare conjunction of cloud and sunlight producing an effect known as *rayons de crépuscule*, or rays of twilight. It is also possible that impressionable children deliberately exaggerated an unusual (but wholly natural) meteorological phenomenon, much in the same spirit that Elsie Wright and Frances Griffith created the celebrated Cottingley fairy photographs, fabricated just a month earlier.

No less dubious was a report in the *Daily News* in February 1930, based on an American newspaper story. According to Colonel Friedrich Herzenwirth, said to be a former member of the German intelligence service:

The Angels of Mons were motion pictures thrown upon 'screens' of foggy white cloudbanks in Flanders by cinematographic projecting machines mounted in German aeroplanes which hovered above the British lines . . . The object of the Germans responsible for these scientific 'visions' was to create superstitious terror in the Allied ranks.

According to Herzenwirth, the plan backfired, and was successfully exploited by the British for their own benefit. However, the very next day the *Daily News* published a corrective report, explaining that its Berlin correspondent had been informed by official German sources that there was no record of the mysterious colonel, whose story was now dismissed as a hoax. Curiously, the projection idea would be resurrected by British propaganda agencies in March 1940, who in the midst of the static Phoney War, gave consideration to 'a suggestion for an apparatus to project images or clouds' over the German lines by means of an unspecified 'magic lantern' apparatus.

The idea was not pursued. However, further evidence of the remarkable staying power of this particular myth came in March 2001, when it was announced that actor Marlon Brando had paid £350,000 for spectral footage of angels shot by William Doidge at Woodchester Park in the Cotswolds during the Second World War. Doidge, a veteran of the BEF and the Retreat from Mons, was said to have been obsessed with the angels legend of 1914, believing they could lead him to his Belgian sweetheart, with whom he had lost contact during the war. Like Machen's original story published by the *Evening News*, the film promised excellent entertainment, although as factual history the verdict is likely to be less kind.

The legend of the Comrade in White is another battlefield myth from the first year of the war which was clearly promulgated to underline the moral and religious rectitude of the Allied cause. As we have seen, the legend of the Bowmen at Mons lay dormant for six months after its initial publication 1914, only to return with more pronounced angelic and religious overtones in April 1915. To those who chose to accept such evidence at face value, further proof that God was on the side of the Allies, rather than Germany, came in the form of the Comrade in White, or white helper, first encountered on the battlefields of the Western Front at more or less the same time.

The first account was given in *Bladud*, described as the Bath Society Paper, in June 1915. According to Dr R.F. Horton, a well-known Congregational minister from Manchester who was also a devout believer in the Angel of Mons:

Now and again a wounded man on the field is conscious of a comrade in white coming with help and even delivering him. One of our men who had heard of this story again and again, and has put it down to hysterical excitement, had an experience. His division had advanced and was not adequately protected by the artillery. It was cut to pieces, and he himself fell. He tried to hide in a hollow of the ground, and as he lay helpless, not daring to lift his head under the hail of fire, he saw One in White coming to him. For a moment he thought it must be a hospital attendant or a stretcher bearer, but no, it could not be; the bullets were flying all around. The White-robed came near and bent over him. The man lost consciousness for a moment, and when he came round he seemed to be out of danger.

The White-robed still stood by him, and the man, looking at his hand, said, 'You are wounded in your hand.' There was a wound in the palm. He answered, 'Yes, that is an old wound that has opened again lately.' The soldier says that in spite of the peril and his wounds he felt a joy he had never experienced in his life before.

A similar account, yet again from an unknown soldier in an unidentified sector, was printed in *Life and Work* magazine in June 1915, from which the following extracts are drawn:

George Casey told me all he knew . . . After many a hot engagement a man in white had been seen bending over the wounded. Snipers sniped at him. Shells fell all around. Nothing had power to touch him. He was either heroic beyond all heroes, or he was something greater still. This mysterious one, whom the French called the Comrade in White, seemed to be everywhere at once. At Nancy, in the Argonne, at Soissons and Ypres, everywhere men were talking of him with hushed voices.

The writer continues, explaining that he had hardly expected such phenomenal help should he be injured in battle. Then, during an advance on the enemy trenches, he was hit in both legs, and lay immobile in a shell crater until nightfall.

The night fell, and soon I heard a step, but quiet and firm, as if neither darkness nor death could check those untroubled feet. So little did I guess what was coming that, even when I saw the gleam of white in the darkness, I thought it was a peasant in a white smock, or perhaps a woman deranged. Suddenly, with a little shiver of joy or fear, I don't know which, I guessed that it was the Comrade in White. And at that very moment the German rifles began to shoot. The bullets could scarcely miss such a target, for he flung his arms out as though in entreaty, and then drew them back till he stood like one of those wayside crosses that we saw so often as we marched through France.

And he spoke. The word sounded familiar, but all I remember was the beginning, 'If thou hadst known,' and the ending, 'but now they are hid from thine eyes.' And then he stopped and ushered me into his arms – me, the biggest man in the regiment – and carried me as if I had been a child. I must have fainted, for I woke to consciousness in a little cave by the stream, and the Comrade in White was washing my wounds and binding them up. It seems foolish to say it, for I was in terrible pain, but I was happier at that moment than ever I remember to have been in all my life before . . . And while he swiftly removed every trace of blood or mire, I felt as if my whole nature was being washed, as if all the grime and soil of sin were going, and as if I were once more a little child.

I suppose I slept, for when I awoke this feeling was gone, I was a man, and I wanted to know what I could do for my friend to help him or to serve him. He was looking towards the stream, and his hands were clasped in prayer: and then I saw that he, too, had been wounded. I could see, as it were, a shot-wound in his hand, and as he prayed a drop of blood gathered and fell to the ground. I cried out. I could not help it, for that wound of his seemed to be a more awful thing than any that bitter war had shown me. 'You are wounded, too,' I said faintly. Perhaps he heard me, perhaps it was the look on my face, but he answered me gently 'This is an old wound, but it has troubled me of late.'

And then I noticed sorrowfully that the same cruel mark was on his feet. You will wonder that I did not know sooner. I wonder myself. But it was only when I saw his feet that I knew him.

Ultimately the Comrade in White seems always to have been identified with Jesus Christ, a fact reflected in contemporary illustrations such as the postcard by G. Hillyard Swinstead (Plate 12). The basic concept has something in common with the more modern conception of near-death experience, which is perhaps explicable by medical science, although the white helper legend is heavily, if attractively, embroidered. The elements of deliverance and moral truth are particularly clear from the inference that Christ's wounds had lately opened, no doubt as a result of Hun bullets and frightfulness. It is interesting, too, that like the resurgent angels in 1915 the story seems to have spread first from the vicinity of Bath and Bristol, rather than the front line, although this may be purely coincidental.

A new twist on the legend of the white helper was published in the American magazine *Fate* in 1968. The author, an American clergyman from Massachusetts, claimed to have been told the story some 12 years earlier by an English engineer, who had been in the line at Ypres in August 1915 during one of the early German poison gas attacks:

> They looked out over No Man's Land and saw a strange grey cloud rolling towards them. When it struck, pandemonium broke out. Men dropped all around him and the trench was in an uproar. Then, he said, a strange thing happened. Out of the mist, walking across No Man's Land, came a figure. He seemed to be without special protection and he wore the uniform of the Royal [Army] Medical Corps (RAMC). The engineer remembered that the stranger spoke English with what seemed to be a French accent.
>
> On his belt the stranger from the poison cloud had a series of small hooks on which were suspended tin cups. In his hand he carried a bucket of what looked like water. As he slid down into the trench he began removing the cups, dipping them into the bucket and passing them out to the soldiers, telling them to drink quickly. The engineer was among those who received the potion. He said it was extremely salty, almost too salty to swallow. But all of the soldiers who were given the liquid did drink it, and not one of them suffered lasting effects from the gas.
>
> When the gas cloud had blown over and things calmed down the unusual visitor was not to be found. No explanation for his visit could be given by the Royal Medical Corps – but the fact

remained that thousands of soldiers died or suffered lasting effects from that grim attack, but not a single soldier who took the cup from the stranger was among the casualties.

The story has few, if any, elements in common with the contemporary reports of the Comrade in White from 1915, and although more scientific in tone is scarcely more credible. Certainly there is no evidence that the story of a miraculous French RAMC orderly with a bucket of brine was in circulation on the Western Front at the time, or indeed reported at all during the war years.

Several accounts which followed in the wake of the legend of bowmen and angels at Mons made reference to remarkable clouds, sometimes glowing, which concealed and delivered British troops from the enemy. Far more notorious, however, is the oft-told legend of the Vanished Battalion, in which mysterious clouds took on a more malevolent aspect. The most well-known version of the tale is set against the background of the ill-starred Gallipoli campaign, and in particular the bitter fighting around Hill 60, near Suvla Bay, in August 1915. According to a report first published in 1965, on August 21st a group of New Zealand sappers watching from trenches on a spur overlooking Hill 60 noted:

Perhaps six or eight 'loaf of bread' shaped clouds – all shaped exactly alike, which were hovering over Hill 60. It was noticed that in spite of a four or five mile an hour breeze from the south, these clouds did not alter their position . . . Also stationary and resting on the ground right underneath this group of clouds was a similar cloud in shape, measuring about 800 feet in length, 220 feet in height, and 200 feet in width. This cloud was absolutely dense, solid-looking in structure, and positioned about 14 to 18 chains from the fighting in British-held territory . . . Its colour was light grey, as was the colour of the other clouds.

The account goes on to relate that a British unit, stated to be the 1st/4th Norfolk Regiment, comprising several hundred men, was noticed marching up a sunken road or creek towards Hill 60:

However when they arrived at this cloud they marched straight into it, with no hesitation, but no-one ever came back out to deploy and fight at Hill 60. About an hour later, after the last of the file had disappeared into it, this cloud very unobtrusively lifted off the ground and . . . rose slowly until it joined the other similar clouds . . . As soon as the singular cloud had risen to their level they all moved away northwards, i.e. towards Thrance [Bulgaria]. In a matter of about three-quarters of an hour they had all disappeared from view.

The written statement was signed by Frederick Reichardt, who served throughout the Gallipoli campaign as a Sapper with the New Zealand Expeditionary Force, and was supported by two other ANZAC veterans named Newnes and Newman. Reichardt's fantastical story was first printed in April 1965 in *Spaceview*, a New Zealand journal, and in March of the following year reached a wider audience courtesy of the American UFO magazine *Flying Saucers*. Since then the myth of the Vanished Battalion has been repeated in countless books and magazines, usually bracketed with supernormal phenomena such as the Bermuda Triangle and unsolved disappearances. Some later re-tellings held that the cloud took the form of a giant cross, although it seems unlikely that divine intervention can be inferred. New heights of silliness were scaled by French writer Jacques Vallée in his book *Passport to Magonia*, which offered the theory that the unit had marched into a cloud which concealed a UFO. A similar theory was advanced by the British ufologist Brinsley le Poer Trench (the Earl of Clancarty) in his book *The Eternal Subject*, published in 1973.

The truth of the matter is less sensational. On August 12th, rather than the 21st, several hundred men of the 1/5th (Territorial) Battalion of the Norfolk Regiment were ordered to clear a valley on the Anafarta Plain of Turkish snipers and machine gun posts, in anticipation of a major British assault scheduled for the following day. The Norfolks were lead by Lieutenant-Colonel Sir Horace Proctor-Beauchamp and were flanked by the 8th Hampshires and the 5th Suffolks. For reasons which remain unclear, the Norfolks turned half right as they advanced, thereby opening up a dangerous gap between them and the rest of the attacking force. While still some way short of the Turkish line, the already exhausted Norfolks fixed bayonets and charged towards Kavak Tepe ridge. The attack faltered on difficult, unfamiliar terrain, and over the next few hours the battalion was decimated by sniper, machine gun and artillery fire. Amidst this unfolding disaster, Colonel Proctor-Beauchamp continued to advance at the head of a party comprising approximately 250 officers and men, only to meet with almost complete annihilation after being cut off at an isolated farm.

In the space of some six hours the strength of the 1/5th Norfolks had been halved to less than 400 men. The disaster was almost certainly due to a combination of poor planning and leadership, and the foolhardy bravery of an untested Territorial battalion determined to prove its worth in combat after just two days ashore. The Norfolks attacked in broad daylight across largely open ground which had not been reconnoitred, against an ill-defined objective, without the aid of adequate maps. The defending Turks were well prepared and dug in, and after surrounding Proctor-Beauchamp's exposed force simply cut them to pieces. The survivors were despatched on the spot in cold blood, with only fourteen taken into captivity.

Why, then, did an enduring legend arise around the 1/5th Norfolks? Following the Battle of Neuve-Chapelle in March 1915, comparable stories circulated that whole battalions disappeared without trace in the Bois de Biez, but these quickly faded from memory. Yet long before wild claims of loaf-shaped clouds and extra-terrestrial abduction entered into circulation, the disappearance of the 1/5th Norfolks at Gallipoli had earned an entirely unwarranted degree of infamy. This was principally because the missing men from the 5th Battalion included a company recruited exclusively from the extensive royal estate at Sandringham, made up of gardeners, gamekeepers, farm labourers and household servants, and led by the King's Agent, Captain Frank Beck. The involvement of the Sandringham Company added considerable weight to a tragedy already given a gloss of mystery by Sir Ian Hamilton, the oft-vilified British Commander-in-Chief at Gallipoli, who had written of the incident in a dispatch to Lord Kitchener:

In the course of the fight there happened a very mysterious thing. . . . The Colonel, with 16 officers and 250 men, still kept pushing on, driving the enemy before him . . . Nothing more was ever seen or heard of any of them. They charged into the forest, and were lost to sight or sound. Not one of them ever came back.

King George V also telegraphed Hamilton about the fate of the Sandringham Company, and following the Armistice there should have been little genuine mystery. As early as the autumn of 1919 a Graves Registration Unit discovered a mass grave on the Anafarta Plain which contained the remains of about 180 British soldiers, no fewer than 122 of them men from the 1/5th Norfolks. The remains of Colonel Proctor-Beauchamp, identifiable by virtue of his distinctive silver insignia, were found to be among them. The spot was about a mile beyond the British front line, and half a mile behind the Turkish line. Controversy lingers as to whether the men had been shot through the head, and therefore massacred after being taken prisoner rather than killed in action, but even this theory is far removed from the general misapprehension that the entire battalion had vanished into thin air.

Whether Sapper Reichardt was guilty of deliberate fabrication is open to question. In his carefully researched account of the loss of the Sandringham Company, *All the King's Men*, author Nigel McCrery charitably suggests that the New Zealander was simply confused. Although on August 21st 1915 there was indeed a major British attack against the Turkish positions on Hill 60, the 5th Norfolks took no part in it, due largely to the heavy losses suffered by the battalion on the 12th. Over the course of the next week more than 3,000 troops were thrown into the attack on the enemy redoubt, including the Sherwood Rangers Yeomanry under Lieutenant-Colonel Sir John Peniston Milbank VC. Prior to their murderous assault the Colonel is said to have remarked to one of his officers:

We are to take a redoubt but I don't know where it is, and I don't think anyone else does either; but in any case we are to go ahead and attack the Turks in any event.

The attack by the Sherwood Rangers, which took place at the time and date identified by Reichardt, was a confused and futile disaster, it being reported that the unit quickly became lost to sight in a thick, unseasonable mist, from which few emerged alive. It was perhaps the destruction of this unit which Reichardt observed, although even this is open to question. Certainly Reichardt cannot have observed the attack of the Norfolks across the Anafarta Plain, which was made over four miles from his vantage point on Rhododendron Spur, and took place on the 12th not the 21st, and was carried out by the 5th Battalion rather than the 4th.

CHAPTER FOUR

The Rape of Belgium

On the morning of August 4th 1914, when the Kaiser's army marched across the Belgian frontier, it did so within living memory of the Franco–Prussian War of 1870. For Germany this short campaign had ended in spectacular victory. Napoleon III was defeated by von Moltke (the elder) within a matter of weeks, and surrendered his field army at Sedan. Yet the battle was far from over. At the instigation of a hastily convened Government of National Defence, some 58,000 French irregulars were organized into so-called *corps-francs*, the purpose of which was to harass the enemy communication lines and attack isolated pockets of German troops. Many of the irregulars wore no uniforms, and were given no quarter when captured. Seventy years later, during the Second World War, their descendants would be feted as the resistance movement. In 1870–71, however, the *corps-francs* were demonized by the Germans as villainous murderers, or *franc-tireurs*.

Later historical research reveals that the *corps-francs* accounted for no more than 1,000 German casualties. More importantly, their guerilla campaign obliged the Germans to divert 120,000 fighting troops to protect their rear lines, a figure which amounted to one-quarter of the total German military strength in France. For the invader the consequences were little short of disastrous, and in 1914 the German General Staff were determined that history should not be repeated. But repeated it was, if the following paragraph from the *Daily News* of August 12th is to be believed:

Lively incidents are reported from Herstal, 20 miles south-east of Liège. When the enemy made his first appearance all its strong-hearted sons were in the trenches before Liège, but the women, many of whom are employed at the National Firearm Factory for which Herstal is famous, had sworn to save the works from falling into the hands of the Germans. They seized revolvers and swords, and when the Uhlans charged up the street threw themselves against the foe with a fury which was superb.

Their ammunition exhausted and their swords struck from their hands, they barricaded themselves in their homes and flung boiling water from the windows over the heads of the German lancers. It is stated that 250 troopers have been placed *hors de combat* through burns. The children and grandfathers helped, and when the enemy was obliged to join the general attack on the forts of Liège, the Belgian flag still flew above Herstal Factory.

According to *The Times* on the same date, no less than 2,000 German Uhlans had been scalded and burned at Herstal. Three weeks later the same paper ran another report of heroic civilian resistance from Belgium, only marginally less sensational:

Boy scouts all over the world will be proud of Georges Leysen, of Liège, a lad of 18, who has been decorated by the King and given a commendation. Young Leysen, by brilliant work, has already a bag of eleven spies, all of whom have been shot. He has killed an Uhlan and captured another at Malines, though suffering from a broken arm. Near Malines two fellow boy scouts of 16 and 17 were executed. Leysen declares their only arm was a long knife. On Sunday morning Leysen, who is the hero of the hour in Antwerp, left with important official dispatches for Brussels. He has already twice pierced the German lines.

Whatever the truth of either story, it is certainly true that at the beginning of August there was a certain amount of sporadic and uncoordinated partisan activity by Belgian civilians and civil guards. On August 30th, for example, several Belgian men confessed to a court in Aachen that they had fired on German troops, and were sentenced to death. From the outset, Germany made it clear that it would not tolerate covert attacks on its forces by civilians, nor any group not properly organized in accordance with the laws and usages of war, and would punish such 'perfidities' as the collective responsibility of the population in the general vicinity. The wholesale destruction of property and the execution of civilian hostages were thus condoned by the German High Command as a blunt yet necessary instrument of policy in the subjugation of occupied territory. In this way, so it was reasoned, an entire nation could be terrorized into absolute submission, with the least possible diversion of military strength. Indeed Clausewitz had prescribed terror as a desirable method to shorten war, his entire methodology being based on the necessity of making war short, sharp and decisive. A word was even coined for the strategy: *Schreklichkeit*, or frightfulness.

Germany appears to have been obsessively concerned with perceived violations of international law, while conveniently ignoring the fact that the very presence of its army on neutral Belgian soil was itself an illegal act of aggression. This obsession was manifest in two main accusations: that Belgian resistance activity was illegal, and that it was endorsed and organized by those in authority, be they government officials, mayors or priests. Indeed German commanders from Ludendorff downward appear to have been only too keen to anticipate, magnify or simply fabricate instances of sniping or physical remonstration in order to set necessary examples. When the German army entered a town, notices were immediately posted warning the population that the mayor, the leading magistrate and the senator of the district would be held as hostages against guerilla attacks, on penalty of death. The taking and killing of hostages was practised systematically, as was the requisitioning of food and livestock, and demands for sureties. The further the Germans advanced, the more hostages were arrested.

The town of Herve was razed as early as the beginning of August, while on the 10th at Linsmeau eleven male villagers were rounded up and shot. On the 15th the town of Visé, on the Dutch frontier, was largely destroyed after reports of sniper fire, although the town had by then been occupied for two weeks. About 38 civilians were killed, and 631 men and boys removed to Germany for forced labour. The remainder of the population, some 4,000 people, fled across the border to Holland. The tragic litany goes on. On the 19th 150 civilians were executed at Malines and another 27 at Aerschot, while on the 20th and 21st the town of Andenne was set ablaze, and up to 200 civilians shot in retaliation for alleged *franc-tireur* attacks. The official German proclamation put the figure at 110, although Belgian accounts estimated the death toll at 211. At Seilles, near Andenne, it was 50, at Monceau-sur-Sambre 40, and on the 22nd at Tamines, 384, after Germans were angered by the stubborn resistance of a French army unit.

This atmosphere of brutality was much aggravated by the fact that German troops were themselves fed stories of outlandish atrocities committed by Belgian civilians, as were their families at home. As early as August 8th the novelist Walter Bloem, then a captain in the 12th Brandenburg Grenadiers, recorded en route to the front:

We bought the morning papers at a wayside station and read, amazed, of the experiences of those of our troops already across the Belgian frontier – of priests, armed, at the head of marauding bands of Belgian civilians, committing every kind of atrocity, and putting the deeds of 1870 into the shade; of treacherous ambushes of patrols, and sentries found later with eyes pierced and tongues cut off, of poisoned wells and other horrors. Such was the first breath of war, full of venom, that, as it were, blew in our faces as we rolled on towards it.

Bloem admitted to being haunted by the 'monstrous thought' that he might be hit by a bullet fired by a civilian, and that during an exhausting march of 28 miles in a single day, not one of his men fell out of line because 'the thought of falling into the hands of the Walloons was worse than sore feet'. As days became weeks, the atrocity reports became increasingly exaggerated on both sides. The

American Ambassador to Belgium, Brand Whitlock, recorded with no little irony that continual German justifications left the impression that the burgomeisters of Belgian towns had bred a special race of children, so often was the reason advanced for a particular atrocity that the son or daughter of the local mayor had attacked an innocent or unarmed German soldier. On September 15th the *Kolnische Volkzeitung* offered that:

> It is proved beyond doubt that German wounded were robbed and killed by the Belgian population and indeed were subject to horrible mutilations, and that even women and young girls took part in these shameful actions. In this way, the eyes of German soldiers were torn out, their ears, noses, fingers and sexual organs cut off or their body cut open.

Other atrocity myths at large in Germany held that troops had been doused with boiling oil at one location, or served with poisoned food at another, or blinded by exploding cigars. It was also said that wounded soldiers had been robbed and killed, and that in Aachen 30 officers lay blinded in hospital, their eyes gouged out by Belgian women and children. A related story told of the discovery of a bucketful of soldiers' eyeballs, a battlefield myth which had its origins in the Crusades. Indeed a large proportion of these reports were merely the stock-in-trade offered by propagandists from previous conflicts, removed from their shelves, dusted down, re-labelled, and sold as new.

In fact two streams of propaganda found themselves in conflict. For a brief period, reports appeared in the Belgian press which arguably provided Germany with some small measure of justification. According to the *Neuwe Gazet* for August 8th 1914:

> At Visé young and old ran to take up arms, and if they were unable to stop the murderous advance of the German cavalry the inhabitants at least resisted until the last moment.

While an Antwerp newspaper, *Metropole*, announced the next day:

Some of the inhabitants of Liège broke open the window of a gunsmith's shop, seized guns, revolvers and cartridges and pursued the Uhlans to the outskirts of the town.

The propaganda of Belgian patriotism was therefore at odds with the propaganda of Belgian innocence. But if these stories can be said to prove anything at all, like the legend of the lethal boy scout Georges Leysen, and the deadly munitionettes at Herstal, it is merely that it is impossible to say whether the Allied or German side first began to promote stories of atrocities in Belgium.

Despite a lack of coherent resistance, as August wore on the level of German frightfulness increased. By far the worst of the massacres took place at Dinant. On August 22nd the right wing of the French 5th Army fell back from the line of the River Meuse below Namur, demolishing several key bridges as they retreated. One such crossing was at Dinant, a picturesque town dominated by a large citadel on top of the steep cliffs on the right bank. The following day the advancing German 3rd Army set about repairing the bridge as quickly as possible, but claimed that Belgian civilians tried to hamper their progress. Their commander, General von Hausen, ordered an immediate reprisal: hundreds of hostages were rounded up, held in the main square until evening, and then shot by firing squad. In all, 612 bodies were identified and buried, the youngest victim being just three weeks old. An official German statement later sought to excuse the killing of women and children (who accounted for one-sixth of the victims) on the basis that they had been caught in crossfire with Belgian army stragglers, or else had refused to be separated from male hostages. Neither explanation is particularly credible, let alone a justification.

More infamous still was the sacking of Louvain over a five-day period between August 26th and 30th. The historic university city had been occupied by the German 1st Army on August 19th, and although a number of prominent citizens were taken hostage, and a cash indemnity demanded, the population were treated in a generally acceptable fashion. The 1st Army then moved on towards Brussels and Mons, to be replaced by IX Reserve Corps. On the 25th an attack by Belgian forces from Antwerp against German positions near Louvain triggered a mild panic amongst the troops in the city, and allegations of *franc-tireur* activity by Belgian civilians. The following day the German military governor of Brussels, General von Luttwitz, pronounced that the German commandant in Louvain had been shot by the son of the town mayor, which was a nonsense, and ordered that Louvain be razed in reprisal. During the extended orgy of violence which followed, about a fifth of the city's houses were gutted, the church of St Pierre badly damaged by fire, and the ancient medieval university library containing 230,000 priceless volumes destroyed. It is not known precisely how many civilians perished, although on the 28th an American diplomat saw blackened buildings, the bodies of civilians and horses in the streets, and German troops – some of them apparently drunk – driving people from their houses in order to complete the destruction.

In the wake of the sacking of Louvain *The Times* described the Germans as 'Huns' for the first time, thereby striking a deathless epithet. Another ostensibly reliable eyewitness description of the pillage of the city was provided by an American journalist, Gerald Morgan:

A hour before sunset we entered Louvain and found the city a smoking furnace. The railway station was crowded with troops, drunk with loot and liquor, and rapine as well. From house to house, acting under orders, groups of soldiers were carrying lighted straw, placing it in the basement, and then passing on to the next. It was not one's idea of a general conflagration, for each house burnt separately – hundreds of individual bonfires – while the sparks shot up like thousands of shooting stars into the still night air . . . Meanwhile, through the station arch we saw German justice being administered. In a square outside, where the cabs stand, an officer stood, and the soldiers drove the citizens of Louvain into his presence, like so many unwilling cattle on a market day. Some of the men, after a few words between the officers and the escorts, were marched off under fixed bayonets behind the railway station. Then we heard volleys, and the soldiers returned. Then the train moved out, and the last we saw of the doomed city was an immense red glare in the gathering dusk.

In its sweep through Belgium, it is thought that the Imperial German Army deliberately or recklessly caused the deaths of as many as 5,000 civilians. As well as mass executions, it is also established fact that on occasion advancing German troops used civilian hostages as a human shield, as at Nimy, north-east of Mons, on August 23rd, when several hundred villagers were forced to screen an attack on a bridge held by men of the Worcestershire Regiment. In addition to acts of this kind, which were officially condoned, it may be taken as read that any army which contained a representative cross-section of society must inevitably include in its ranks certain brutal and perverted individuals. Given the circumstances of the German invasion of Belgium and France, it was inevitable that ample opportunity would arise for such individuals to give rein to their passions.

Remarkably, at no time did Germany seek to conceal the nature or extent of any so-called reprisals, and foreign journalists were left free to report them as warnings. This policy of openness was wholly misguided, and would quickly backfire with catastrophic results on the international stage. Nevertheless, in seeking to justify the sacking of Louvain, official sources in Berlin repeated the core rationale behind their policy of *Schreklichkeit*:

The distribution of arms and ammunition among the civil population of Belgium has been carried out on systematic lines, and the authorities enraged the public against Germany by assiduously circulating false reports. The only means of preventing surprise attacks from the civil population has been to interfere with unrelenting severity and to create examples which, by their frightfulness, would be a warning to the whole country.

During August and September 1914 pamphlet and newspaper reports of essentially factual atrocities such as at Dinant and Louvain were rapidly churned and exaggerated. True, criminal acts of arson, theft and hostage murder had been widespread, and certain localities had been put to fire and sword. However graver myths and fictions grew and multiplied, so that in the popular mind the German invasion of Belgium came to be seen as a bestial chronicle of wanton destruction, drunken pillage, religious desecration, hostage and child murder, living burials, perverse mutilation and rape. It mattered little that all too many of these same atrocity stories had been widely circulated in previous wars. At one stroke the German army – jack-booted, spike-helmeted – was re-cast as the ancient Hun, leaving behind a trail of blood, depravity and ruin. German civilians were said to be no more civilized, and women were said to wear necklaces made out of eyes plucked from French wounded. And so forth, ad nauseam, as hysteria darkened into hatred.

Scepticism, where displayed, was likely to be branded as unpatriotic, while for those who were determined to believe, the lack of verifiable evidence was conveniently explicable: the victims had died, or were trapped inside enemy-occupied territory. Lurid stories of German atrocities in Belgium and France were actively promoted by the Allies for a number of reasons. For the Allied governments, they possessed a potent propaganda value, particularly in America, and also boosted collective moral indignation as well as recruitment to the colours. Prior to the introduction of conscription in 1917, the million men who joined Kitchener's New Armies volunteered to fight for a country and a cause, even if ultimately they ended up fighting for their lives. Of equal importance was the fact that Britain had based its entry into the war on the fulfilment of its treaty obligations to Belgium, so any issue which continued to provide justification – both political and moral – for the conflict with Germany was vigorously promoted. For certain lower regions of the fourth estate, atrocity reports also provided an opportunity to run countless items of lurid and exploitative copy which would have been unprintable in peacetime. Strict War Office censorship also meant that there was an almost total lack of official war reporting from the Front, with the result that anecdote and rumour were seldom countered, and allowed to run wild. In an age far less media-literate than our own, in which the public were far less ready to accept that statesmen and editors might knowingly perpetrate falsehoods, propaganda offered ready-made opinions for the unthinking herd.

In Britain, the *Daily News* emerged as one of the tabloid papers least averse to publishing purple atrocity stories. On August 21st, for example:

A woman was forced to undress amid the insults of the soldiers and was then shot. The mayor's wife was shot in her house and the body burned with her home. An old man of 74, deaf and blind, received two volleys in his body. Another was dragged on to the market place and tortured till he died.

And five days later, on the 26th:

An old man . . . had his arm sliced in three longitudinal cuts; he was then hung head downwards and burned alive. Young girls have been raped and little children outraged, and at Orsmeal several inhabitants suffered mutilations too horrible to describe.

On October 14th the same paper carried the story of yet another boy scout shot by Uhlans for refusing to give information about the French army. The content of atrocity reports swiftly became generic. The characteristic story was supplied by an anonymous correspondent some distance from the scene of the crime, and invariably took the form of a supposedly verbatim account by an unidentified 'Belgian soldier' or 'married woman', albeit delivered second- or third-hand. Descriptions of cruelties to women, children and the elderly predominated, and chimed with the standard depiction of Belgium itself as the violated maiden, taken by force, then mutilated horribly and left to die. In France, the Bureau de la Presse released atrocity stories in such quantities that the French press ceased to report them under individual headlines, and instead ran them week after week beneath the same heading: *Les Atrocitiés Allemandes*.

Other factual incidents were also reported in Allied and neutral papers as comparable examples of Hunnish barbarity. On August

25th several bombs or shells landed on Antwerp, causing perhaps
a dozen civilian casualties. It was said to be the first Zeppelin
bombing raid of the war, and as such was widely reported, not
least because bombardment by airships had long been anticipated
with much the same level of dread as atomic attack a half century
later. An American journalist present in the port, E. Alexander
Powell, filed a gory report on the aftermath, describing in detail
how one policeman had had both his legs blown off, and how the
head of a woman watching from a window was severed. Powell
entered one house to inspect the room where a woman had been
sleeping:

> She had literally been blown to fragments. The floor, the walls, the
> ceilings were splotched with – well, it's enough to say that the
> woman's remains could only have been collected with a shovel.

Over the next twelve months this litany of infamies would be
extended to include the shelling of Rheims Cathedral in September,
the callous bombardment of Scarborough and Hartlepool by German
warships in December (leaving 137 dead and 592 wounded), the
declaration of unrestricted submarine warfare in February 1915, the
first use of poison gas near Ypres in April, the sinking of the Cunard
liner *Lusitania* in May with the loss of over 1,000 lives, and the
execution of Edith Cavell in October. One by one these successive
outrages served only to endorse Lloyd George's pronouncement of
September 14th 1914 that 'the new philosophy of Germany is to
destroy Christianity'.

Against this background it was hardly surprising that atrocity
propaganda was also spread from the pulpit. In October 1914 one
clergyman informed the Manchester Geographical Society that:

> You will hear only a hundredth part of the actual atrocities this
> war has produced. The civilized world could not stand the truth. It
> will never hear it. There are, up and down England today, scores –
> I am understating this number – of Belgian girls who have had
> their hands cut off. That is nothing to what we could tell you.

Others were only too keen to tell more, although all too often these 'truths' were little more than hysterical and even pornographic fantasies. Witness the following letter published in *The Times* on September 12th, submitted by a London vicar and supposedly quoting verbatim from a letter from a BEF officer at the Front:

> We have got three girls in the trenches with us who came to us for protection. One had no clothes on, having been outraged by the Germans . . . Another poor girl has just come in having had both her breasts cut off. I caught the Uhlan officer in the act, and with a rifle at three hundred yards, killed him.

Another BEF officer, Major A. Corbett-Smith of the Royal Field Artillery, offered an even more grotesque account. On August 26th 1914, following a successful British counter-attack on an unnamed town, the major related that:

> Up the main street everywhere was horrible evidence that *they* had been at work. Mingled with dead and wounded combatants were bodies of women and children, many terribly mutilated . . . But there was one thing which, for the men who saw it, dwarfed all else. Hanging up in the open window of a shop, strung from a hook in the cross-beam, like a joint in a butcher's shop, was the body of a little girl, five years old, perhaps. Its poor little hands had been hacked off, and through the slender body were vicious bayonet stabs.

Both these military accounts are almost certainly untrue. Corbett-Smith fails to identify the location, and in describing British units re-taking any town by dint of a combined infantry and cavalry attack his account does not correspond with any known BEF action on the 26th. The Major was a prolific author, and his later war memoirs only add weight to the suspicion that he was simply doing the bidding of the propaganda bureau. However, at a time when war correspondents were treated as outlaws, much war reporting originated in letters from combatants at the front, and a significant percentage of the population accepted such reports without demur.

One of the more notorious amputation stories concerned a Scottish nurse from Dumfries. On September 16th the *Dumfries Standard* reported the story of 23-year-old Grace Hume, who was said to have left home upon the outbreak of the war to serve in a Belgian military hospital at Vilvoorde. When the Germans arrived on September 6th they burnt the hospital, beheaded and killed wounded men, and cut off Nurse Hume's right breast, leaving her to die in agony. A hastily scribbled note reached her younger sister in Dumfries, apparently written as Grace lay dying. The story was widely repeated in several national newspapers, and grew in the telling: a letter from a second nurse from the same hospital, named Millard, was quickly produced, which told how Grace Hume had shot a German who attacked one of her patients, and how her left breast had also been amputated. Delving deeper into the affair, on September 18th *The Times* revealed not only that Nurse Millard did not exist, but that Grace Hume was in fact alive and well and working in Huddersfield, never having left the country. It transpired that the whole story was a fiction concocted by her younger sister Kate, aged 17, who was subsequently reported to have been greatly affected by the loss of their musician brother John on board the *Titanic* in 1912.

On September 30th the unhappy young woman was charged with uttering a forged letter and remanded in custody, and two months later convicted at Dumfries High Court. At trial her doctor ventured the opinion that Hume had read so many stories of German atrocities she had actually come to believe her elder sister had been killed. The jury recommended leniency, and the judge released her immediately on the basis that she had already served three months in prison. The verdict met with widespread approval, although *The Times* still found time to wonder whether the hoax had been part of a German plot to discredit all reports of atrocities. German papers, quite naturally, reported the unravelling of the sorry story with undisguised glee.

In addition to the 100 or so spy dramas produced in British theatres between 1914 and 1918, a number of atrocity plays were also submitted to the Lord Chamberlain's office. *In the Hands of the*

Hun (1915) offered as its villain a sadistic German officer, Count Otto, who planned to burn down a convent and offer the nuns to his men, a fate also threatened by a German naval captain in *For Those in Peril* the following year. Although these plays were produced, certain cuts were demanded, including a scene from *In the Hands of the Hun* in which the Mother Superior was stripped to the waist and then whipped. Also censored was *War, Red War* (1915), in which a German colonel called for a baby to have its brains dashed out on a doorpost, then thrown on a fire. *Armageddon* (1915) is judged to have been one of the better examples of the genre, although *The Times* reviewer noted that the propaganda content might as well have been marked off a checklist: 'Pictures of German barbarity and "frightfulness" – prisoners shot, women insulted, interceding priests mocked, and so forth . . . German sentiments about world power declaimed.'

Prior to May 1915, it is probably true to say that in Britain a degree of scepticism surrounded Belgian atrocity stories. A Belgian writer complained in a book published in 1915 that when he first arrived in London the previous autumn, every atrocity story was considered suspect. Another telling sidelight is thrown by the Reverend Andrew Clark, whose diary entry for October 12th 1914 records:

The Germans in their attack on Belgian villages had really much provocation. At the first arrival of the Germans the regular Belgian forces made themselves scarce, but when the German troops began to enter the village, Belgian girls of 15 or 16, revolver in hand, rushed out into the street and shot down Germans. When the Germans defended themselves, their action was exaggerated and misrepresented.

Even with the benefit of hindsight, it is difficult to comprehend why atrocity stories were so widely believed on the basis of such slender evidence. As early as September 1914, five American journalists who had spent two weeks with the German armies in Belgium had issued a signed declaration that they were unable to substantiate 'a single wanton brutality' – as distinct from hostage executions. None of the men ever revoked the statement, as one might have expected had it been made simply to maintain accreditation. In 1917, a United Press correspondent named William Shepherd made much the same point:

> I was in Belgium when the first atrocity stories went out. I hunted and hunted for atrocities during the first days of the atrocity scare. I couldn't find atrocities. I couldn't find people who had seen them. I travelled on trains with Belgians who had fled from the German lines and I spent much time amongst Belgian refugees. I offered sums of money for photographs of children whose hands had been cut off or who had been wounded or injured in other ways. I never found a first-hand Belgian atrocity story; and when I ran down second-hand stories they all petered out.

Lord Northcliffe offered £200 for an authentic photograph of a mutilated civilian, but the prize was never claimed, and an interested English bishop drew a similar blank. The few photographs which were printed proved to be fakes. One in the *Daily Mirror* for August 25th 1915 depicted three grinning Uhlans 'loaded with gold and silver loot'. In fact the photo was a pre-war picture of three riders who had won cups in the army steeplechase at Grunewald. In France, *Le Monde Illustré* transformed a picture of demonstrations in Berlin over the declaration of war into supposed celebration over the sinking of the *Lusitania*. In any event, cartoons filled the gap, the Allies proving masters of an art form which the Germans were never able to perfect.

More than any other factor, however, the myth of the rape of Belgium came to be accepted as fact following the publication of the infamous Bryce Report in May 1915. The previous December, the very same month in which the unfortunate Kate Hume was convicted, the government had appointed an investigative Committee on Alleged German Outrages. Their eventual report took its name from its chairman, Lord Bryce, an establishment figure who should have been well qualified for the task. As well as being a respected professor of jurisprudence and a noted historian, James Bryce (1838–1922) was a member of the House of Lords, having sat for 26 years as an MP, eight of these as Chief Secretary for Ireland, and nine (1907–13) as a highly popular Ambassador to the United States. There he was spoken of as 'Wilson's old friend', the *St Louis Republican* offering that: 'If there is a man in the entire British Empire whom the people of this nation are prepared to believe implicitly, it is James Bryce.' Ironically, Bryce had also received doctorates from several German universities, and was a recipient of the Order of Pour le Merité, the highest honour within the gift of the Kaiser. The other six members of the Committee comprised three lawyers, two historians and an editor. Its brief was to consider written witness statements and other documents, including the eight separate reports on alleged German atrocities offered up by the Belgian government since August 1914.

The Bryce Report was published in May 1915, just seven days after the sinking of the *Lusitania*, and was translated into 30 languages. In Britain the 360-page volume cost just 1*d* – the price of a newspaper – and was an immediate bestseller. Yet although it had a deliberate and critical influence on public opinion at home and abroad, the enquiry was hugely flawed. It was based largely on depositions taken from 1,200 Belgian refugees, whose evidence was not given under oath, and who were not identified in the published Report. The Committee members themselves did not trouble to travel to Belgium or France, and by relying on a team of 22 barristers to take the statements were spared the burden of actually interviewing a single witness firsthand and assessing the reliability of their accounts for themselves. Hearsay evidence was accepted at face value, and early warnings about the reliability of much of it ignored. Even before the end of December 1914, Bryce himself had been warned that no children with amputated hands had been seen or heard of at any of six given addresses in London, while another source confirmed much the same of girls said to have been made pregnant by rape.

The final report was presented in the format and with the precision of a legal brief. It concluded that a deliberate campaign of terror had been conducted by the German army in Belgium, including organised massacres and arson as well as isolated rapes, murders and assorted outrages. Although these generalities had a basis in truth, the form in which the report's final conclusion was presented in effect endorsed each and every atrocity report to have emerged from Belgium:

It is proved
i. That there were in many parts of Belgium deliberate and systematically organized massacres of the civil population, accompanied by many isolated murders and other outrages.
ii. That in the conduct of the war generally innocent civilians, both men and women, were murdered in large numbers, women violated, and children murdered.
iii. That looting, house burning and the wanton destruction of property were ordered and countenanced by the officers of the German Army, that elaborate provisions had been made for systematic incendiarism at the very outbreak of the war, and that the burnings and destruction were frequent where no military necessity could be alleged, being indeed part of a system of general terrorization.
iv. That the laws and usages of war were frequently broken, particularly by the using of civilians, including women and children, as a shield for advancing forces exposed to fire, to a less degree by killing the wounded and prisoners, and in the frequent abuse of the Red Cross and the White Flag. . .
Murder, lust and pillage prevailed over many parts of Belgium on a scale unparalleled in any war between civilized nations during the last three centuries.

Still more damaging was the appendix, which reproduced 500 of the unsworn, untested depositions. As well as re-heating endless hackneyed tales churned time and again during the preceding nine months, the appendix was the origin of many of the most gruesome atrocity myths destined to remain in circulation long after the end of the war. Its offered details of how German officers and men had publicly raped 20 Belgian girls in the market place at Liège, how eight German soldiers had bayoneted a two-year-old child, and how another had sliced off the breasts of a peasant girl at Malines. Babies had been dipped in boiling water, or spitted on bayonets, or swung against brick walls. When not busy cutting hands off children, or giving them grenades to play with, Germans had vandalized houses and excreted on personal possessions. Crimes against military personnel were also alleged, including the use of dum-dum bullets, the killing of wounded and prisoners, and abuses of Red Cross and white flags. There were even suggestions of cannibalism. The following extract is typical:

> As I looked into the kitchen I saw the Germans seize the baby out of the arms of the farmer's wife. There were three German soldiers, one officer and two privates. The two privates held the baby and the officer took out his sword and cut the baby's head off. . . We saw the officer say something to the farmer's wife, and saw her push him away. After five or six minutes the two soldiers seized the woman and put her on the ground. She resisted them and they then pulled all her clothes off until she was quite naked. The officer then violated her while one soldier held her by the shoulders and the other by the arms. After the officer each soldier in turn violated her, the other soldier holding her down. . . After the woman had been violated by the three the officer cut off the woman's breasts.

A Belgian soldier told how women were publicly raped in the market place at Liège:

> Immediately after the men had been killed, I saw the Germans going into the houses in the Place and bringing out the women and girls. About 20 were brought out. They were marched close to the corpses. Each of them was held by the arms. They tried to get away. They were made to lie on tables which had been brought into the square. About 15 of them were then violated. Each of them was violated by about 12 soldiers. While this was going on

about 70 Germans were standing round the women including five young officers. The officers started it. . . The ravishing went on for about one and a half hours. I watched the whole time. Many of the women fainted and showed no sign of life.

One of the most repugnant stories, frequently quoted in the press as 'the foulest crime of three centuries', told of the bayonetting of a small child at Malines:

As the German soldiers came along the street I saw a small child, whether a boy or a girl I could not see, come out of a house. The child was about two years of age. The child came into the middle of the street so as to be in the way of the soldiers. The soldiers were walking in twos. The first line of two passed the child; one of the second line, the man on the left, stepped aside and drove his bayonet with both hands into the child's stomach. Lifting the child into the air on his bayonet and carrying it away on his bayonet, he and his comrades still singing. . . The child screamed when the soldier struck it with his bayonet, but not afterwards.

And so forth. Under the totality principle adopted by Bryce, no lie was too great, and no distortion too bizarre. As an exercise in anti-German propaganda the Report was an unparalled success, and was rushed into print early to capitalize on the sinking of the *Lusitania* on May 7th 1915. Publication and distribution had been arranged by the propaganda department at Wellington House, whose internal press report observed with triumph that:

Even in papers hostile to the Allies, there is not the slightest attempt to impugn the correctness of the facts alleged. Lord Bryce's prestige in America put scepticism out of the question, and many leading articles begin on this note.

C.F.G. Masterman, the head of the British propaganda bureau, wrote in a letter to Bryce on June 7th:

Your report has swept America. As you probably know even the most sceptical declare themselves converted, just because it is signed by you!

Coming hard on the heels of the *Lusitania* tragedy, and the debut of poison gas on the battlefield at Ypres, the report and its lurid appendix triggered the appearance of a fresh wave of atrocity stories in the papers. A set of more or less identical allegations were collated by the French Ministry of Foreign Affairs, and published in Britain at about the same time. All of which raises the question of why an honourable man such as Lord Bryce chose to sign off such a morally questionable document. Bryce no doubt saw the report as his contribution at a time when, in the name of its dead and wounded, every combatant nation realised its future would be signed and sealed by victory or defeat. Had his report concluded that Germany had perpetrated fewer acts of violence than alleged, Bryce perhaps feared undermining Britain's moral justification for fighting Germany. Bryce and his colleagues stopped short of producing a fraudulent report, in that the conclusions drawn were sound based on the selective evidence they chose to examine. But the Committee did take particular care to avoid verifying that evidence. Bearing this in mind, some might share the view of the American observer H.C. Peterson, who concluded in his 1939 study *Propaganda for War* that in perpetuating a fictive litany of ultraviolent and pornographic fantasies, the Bryce Report stood as a *bona fide* atrocity in itself.

Bryce was parroted in a widely read book compiled by J.H. Morgan, *German Atrocities – An Official Investigation*, published in 1916. The title was misleading, in that the 'official' element was a reference to Lord Bryce, not Morgan, although Bryce gave the book his blessing in the *Westminster Gazette*, pronouncing that 'ample justification exists for publishing the horrible record which this book contains'. Based largely on material taken from the infamous appendix, but abandoning all pretence of moderation, Morgan devoted considerable space to the perceived 'bestiality' of German officers and men:

The public has been shocked by the evidence, accepted by the Committee as genuine, which tells of such mutilations of women and children as only the Kurds of Asia Minor had been thought capable of perpetrating. . . The Committee hint darkly at perverted sexual instinct. Cases of sodomy and of the rape of little children did undoubtedly occur on a very large scale. Some of the worst things have never been published. . . There is very strong reason to suspect that young girls were carried off to the trenches by licentious German soldiery, and there abused by hordes of savages and licentious men. . . A girl was found lying naked on the ground 'pegged out' in the form of a crucifix. I need not go on with this chapter of horrors.

As regards private property, respect for it among the German troops simply does not exist. By the universal testimony of every British officer and soldier whom I have interrogated the progress of German troops is like a plague of locusts over the land. . . Cases of petty larceny by German soldiers appear to be innumerable; they take whatever seizes their fancy, and leave the towns they evacuate laden like peddlers. . . Châteaux or private houses used as head-quarters of German officers were frequently found to have been left in a state of bestial pollution, which can only be explained by gross drunkenness or filthy malice. Whichever be the explanation, the fact remains that, while to use the beds and the upholstery of private houses as a latrine is not an atrocity, it indicates a state of mind sufficiently depraved to commit one.

Another popular atrocity text, published in 1917, was *The Marne and After* by Major Corbett-Smith, which devoted an entire chapter to frightfulness and 'Kultur', although his earlier fiction concerning the child on the meat-hook was not included.

The defence offered by Germany to these largely mythical charges was wholly inadequate, and continued to seek to justify frightfulness on the dry basis of violations of international law. In March 1915, two months before the publication of the Bryce Report, Berlin issued its own 'White Book' of sworn testaments to alleged murders and mutilations of German troops by Belgian soldiers and civilians. In addition to the alleged *franc-tireur* attacks described at the beginning of this chapter, priests were said to have gunned down German soldiers from behind altars, and served poisoned food and drink, while women and children were accused of having maimed German wounded, assassinated officers in their quarters at night, and even carried out crucifixions. German civilians were also said to have endured unwarranted cruelties on the outbreak of war.

In terms of content, these stories equalled those of the Allies – or All-Lies, as Berlin suggested – yet had nothing like the same impact on international opinion. German propaganda to neutral territories was, in general, less effective than that produced by Britain and France, failing as it did to simplify the issues of the war into right against wrong. Germany also failed to establish any coordinated machine for propaganda, and was much disadvantaged at an early stage when the British cable ship *Telconia* cut her deep sea cables off Emden on August 5th 1914, thus severing Germany's main line of communication to America. To many, the Rape of Belgium became the supreme issue of the war, and the 'precipitant' of opinion across the Atlantic. Matthias Erzberger, later the Kaiser's Chief of Propaganda, concluded that events such as the sacking of Louvain 'aroused almost the entire world' against Germany. The stock counter-argument, that the conduct of German commanders and troops was justified by law and military necessity, was woefully inadequate.

In addition, Germany was greatly handicapped by the paucity of factual incidents which could be suitably spun. The shooting of a dozen survivors of the crew of *U27* by marines from the British Q-ship *Baralong* on August 19th 1915 was probably as close as it came. The episode became public after crew members from an American vessel voiced their misgivings to the State Department. After being re-named *Wiarda*, the *Baralong* repeated this performance five days later upon the *U41*, running down two crewmen who had crawled into a lifeboat. Germany's predictable response was to demand that Britain 'take proceedings for murder' against *Baralong*'s commander and crew. Britain noted with irony the sudden concern by her enemy for the principles of civilized warfare, while at the same time observing that the charges were negligible compared with other crimes 'deliberately committed by German officers . . . against combatants and non-combatants'. In fact this ignominious episode had been carried out in accordance with standing Admiralty instructions, drafted by Winston Churchill, by which German submarine crews were to be treated as 'felons' without any of the rights accorded to prisoners of war. 'Survivors,' wrote the ebullient First Lord, 'should be taken prisoner or shot – whichever is most convenient.'

After the crew of Zeppelin *L19* were left to drown in the North Sea by the crew of the Grimsby trawler *King Stephen* in February 1916, similar German efforts to build a propaganda sensation were stillborn. Germany also tried to counter Allied propaganda by providing neutral papers with stories and photographs of favourable German activity in occupied territory, or of the warm welcome offered to the Kaiser's army by Belgian civilians. By these accounts, German soldiers were forever rescuing Belgian children from flooded streams and deep canals. However, positive reports were far less newsworthy than the sensationalist fare served up by the Allies, which reached a peak in the wake of Bryce. There was no better illustration of German mishandling and naiveté than the case of Edith Cavell in October 1915. The 'martyrdom' of Cavell caught the imagination of artists and newspapers alike, although a great deal of factual information was withheld from the public. As a matron running a training hospital in Brussels, she had, since early in the war, been involved in running an underground network which helped Allied prisoners escape across the Dutch frontier. She knew well enough that her penalty if caught would be death, espionage being a capital offence within the laws and usages of war. Indeed by the time Cavell was shot by firing squad the French had already executed one German woman, Marguerite Schmidt, for precisely the same offence, and by the end of the war had executed several more, Mata Hari included. Nevertheless, the execution of Cavell caused an outcry, typified by the words of the Bishop of London to a crowd in Trafalgar Square:

The cold-blooded murder of Miss Cavell, a poor English girl, deliberately shot by the Germans for housing refugees, will run the sinking of the *Lusitania* close in the civilized world as the greatest crime in history.

A similar double standard applied to the shocked publicity surrounding a photograph of an Austrian trench club, exhibited as representing 'culture at the stage of cannibalism', while making no mention of the fact that similar weapons were used by Allied troops, and even manufactured on a commercial basis by British firms. Later on in the war some alleged atrocity victims also turned their (remaining) hands to commerce of a macabre kind. An American artillery lieutenant with the AEF's 32nd Division recalled an unpleasant scene as his men disembarked at Brest in March 1918:

> One Belgian youngster, about twelve, made a good thing by exciting the pity of the Americans by showing his wounds, which he said were from German atrocities. He had an inch-long scar in his tongue, caused, he said, by a German soldier piercing it with a bayonet. On his back was a mass of scar tissue and blackened skin, about six inches across, which must have been caused by a severe burn. There had been so much publicity in the States about German atrocities, real or alleged, that most of us accepted the Belgian stories as truth at the time.

The point being that a bayonet wound through the tongue alone seems highly unlikely. Although Germany bore the brunt of these charges, she was not alone. All the Central Powers were the target of Allied hate propaganda, which posited a 'league of scientific savagery' between the Teuton and the Turk. The same kind of allegations were made about the war on the Eastern Front as at Sabac in Serbia, where civilians were massacred by invading Austrian forces. In contrast with the unreliable stories from Belgium and France, there appears to have been no shortage of photographic evidence, if the report published in 1916 is anything to go by. Falsehoods remained a commonplace, however, for example a story from May 1915 that Austrians had killed thousands of Serbian civilians with clouds of poison gas. Nevertheless, the genocidal Turkish massacre of more than a million Armenians between 1915 and 1917 received nothing like the same level of coverage as events in the west, and triggered little by way of moral indignation.

Belief in the falsehood of the more extreme atrocity myths became widespread only in the years after 1918. In his study *The Great War and Modern Memory*, Paul Fussell claimed that an incalculable number of Jews died in the Holocaust 'because of the ridicule during the twenties and thirties . . . about Belgian nuns violated and children sadistically used'. Due to the scepticism engendered by Allied propaganda, Fussell concludes, most people refused to fully credit reports about the death camps until hard evidence emerged in 1945, by which time it was too late. While it is impossible to gauge the truth of this suggestion, it is certainly the case that the extent to which both the troops and the public were duped during the First World War caused a considerable degree of anger, best summed up by Arthur Ponsonby in 1928:

> Finding now that elaborately and carefully staged deceptions were practised on them, they feel a resentment which has not only served to open their eyes but may induce them to make their children keep their eyes open when the next bugle sounds.

In 2001 the Rape of Belgium sounded a curious echo, after a senior German minister offered the first public apology for the massacre at Dinant. During a visit to the town on May 7th the German Secretary of State for Defence, Walter Kolbow, abandoned all allegations of *franc-tireur* provocation, and instead announced with no little humility:

> Eighty-seven years have passed since German soldiers indulged in murder, desecrated churches and torched your residential areas. I would like to ask you all for your forgiveness.

A wreath was then laid by Herr Kolbow at the memorial to the 674 civilian victims, but many locals boycotted the sombre ceremony, including the mayor of Sambreville, whose ward includes the massacre sites at Tamines and Auvelais. The nearby town of Andenne afterwards responded with a demand for payment of £40,000 in respect of each of its victims, 256 in all, to be paid to their surviving descendants. Under Belgian law, it was argued, an apology is akin to an admission of guilt. However, the request was politely turned down by Berlin.

CHAPTER FIVE

Trench Myths

The principal trench and battlefield myths examined in this chapter are those of the Crucified Canadian in 1915, and the German corpse conversion plant, which first gained widespread currency two years later. However, a number of less celebrated legends are worthy of mention in passing.

The first, from August 1914, was that the BEF had suffered extinction-level casualties in France. The story spread almost as soon as British troops started to disembark in France on the 8th, and rapidly gained currency on the Home Front to include fearful losses and packed hospital ships, as well as German victories and insurrection in Paris. On August 14th, London diarist Michael McDonagh noted that 'the most disquieting stories' had been circulating for several days, including the secret nocturnal return of 'thousands' of British casualties to hospitals in London, where the staff had been sworn to 'keep their mouths shut'. Also current were stories of a great naval battle off the coast of Holland, said by some to have resulted in catastrophic losses for the Royal Navy and the death of Admiral Jellicoe. The dockyards at Portsmouth and Chatham were said to be crowded with disabled war vessels. None of this was true, but on August 15th the Press Bureau felt obliged to circulate a statement:

The public are warned against placing the slightest reliance on the many rumours that are current daily regarding alleged victories and defeats, and the arrival of wounded men or disabled ships in this country. They are without exception baseless.

But still the rumours grew. The Reverend Andrew Clark recorded a variant at the end of the month:

August 31st: The morning postman recorded a great scare in Chelmsford on Sunday. An Ichabod telegram had been received there (founded on the reports with which *The Times* Sunday issue had been hoaxed, as I judged) telling that the British army had perished and that France was beaten. The 'wire' was so full of despair that Chelmsford people could not take their tea.

On September 1st the *Daily News* reported on a 'riot of rumours' from France, including 'weird' reports from a returning British holiday-maker named Angell:

Among the English troops there were rumours just as weird. A very widespread one was that the defence of the Liège forts was not made by Belgians at all, but by English soldiers dressed in Belgian uniforms who had been sent over some months ago.

Some rumours were witty, such as that which held that the British Government paid rent to the French for the use of their trenches, and that the men of the Machine Gun Corps routinely fired off belts of ammunition to heat water in the cooling jacket of the Vickers gun for making tea. The Reverend Clark notes another unlikely tale in 1914, this time regarding glistening silk ties worn by officers:

November 9th: The Colonel told Mrs Gale that the reason why so many officers were picked off by the Germans is because of their silk ties. These officers, to prevent them being conspicuous objects, were forbidden to wear belts in action. But while the mens' tunics were buttoned close up under the chin, the tunics of the officers had a slight collar opening at the neck, and behind that opening a silk tie. Although this tie was khaki-colour, the glistening of the silk stuff was noticeable, even at a distance.

More sinister was the legend of the elusive German officer-spy, said to appear in British trenches shortly before an attack was launched. The figure was often described as being dressed in the uniform of a major, but tended to arouse suspicion on account of some small but significant sartorial *faux pas*. From where he came, or to where he returned, was never established, and in some respects this mythic figure can be seen as an opposite to the benign Comrade in White, examined in Chapter Three. Edmund Blunden, in *Undertones of War*, recalled the following encounter:

> A stranger in a soft cap and a trench coat approached, and asked me the way to the German lines. This visitor facing the east was white-faced as a ghost, and I liked neither his soft cap nor the mackintosh nor the right hand concealed under his coat. I, too, felt myself grow pale, and I thought it was as well to direct him down the communication trench . . . at that juncture deserted; he scanned me, deliberately, and quickly went on. Who he was, I have never explained to myself; but in two minutes the barrage was due, and his chances of doing us harm (I thought he must be a spy) were all gone.

A dubious major was encountered by machine gunner George Coppard during the Battle of Loos in 1915:

> I remember during the Loos battle seeing a very military-looking major complete with a monocle, and wearing a white collar. He asked me the way to Hay Alley and spoke good English. I never suspected that anything was wrong, through I was puzzled about his collar, as all our officers were then wearing khaki collars. Shortly after there was a scare, and officers dashed about trying to find the gallant major, but he had vanished.

Yet another suspicious major is retailed by Reginald Grant, a Canadian artillery sergeant, whose embroidered memoir *SOS Stand*

To! was published in New York in 1918. As well as recording several tall spy stories, including the shooting of the station master at Poperinge for signalling to the German lines, and treachery by Belgian women with carrier pigeons, Grant tells of two officers who appeared at his battery position, some distance behind the front line:

> It was during the stay of my battery on the Lens-Arras road, during the Vimy Ridge preparation, that I again personally encountered Fritz in the form of his spy system. One night after the guns had been oiled and prepared for their next job, and we were all busy cleaning up the ammunition for the work in hand, I was accosted by a couple of British officers, a Captain and a Major . . . There was something that told me all was not well with these men . . .
>
> The very next morning after inspection, orders were read and in the instructions were explicit descriptions of two British officers who were German agents and who were making the rounds of the lines, picking up information wherever they could . . . The following night they were spotted in a French estaminet, by a bunch of sharp-eyed Tommies . . . Like a flash both men drew their revolvers, but before they had a chance to use them, the entire bunch was on top of them, and it was a somewhat mussed up Major and Captain that appeared before the OC at the headquarters of the Tommies who sleuthed them.

Another trench myth concerned the supposed existence of bands of lawless deserters in No Man's Land. According to Osbert Sitwell, the outlaws included French, Italian, German, Austrian, Australian, Canadian and English personnel:

> During four long years, furthermore, the sole internationalism – if it existed – had been that of deserters from all the warring nations . . . Outlawed, these men lived – at least, they lived! – in caves and grottoes under certain parts of the front line . . . They would issue forth, it was said, from their secret lairs after each of the interminable check-mate battles, to rob the dying of their few

possessions – treasures such as boots or iron-rations – and leave them dead. Were these bearded figures, shambling in rags and patched uniforms . . . a myth created by suffering among the wounded, as a result of pain, privation and exposure, or did they exist? It is difficult to tell. At any rate, the story was widely believed among the troops, who maintained that the General Staff could find no way of dealing with these bandits until the war was over, and that in the end they had to be gassed.

A cavalry officer, Ardern Beaman, told a similar story in 1920 in his memoir *The Squadroon*. In 'The Devastated Area', a chapter dealing with a fruitless search for an escaped German prisoner in the spring of 1917, Beaman describes an encounter with an army salvage unit at work on the battlefields of the Somme:

> At Fresnes on the borders of this horrid desolation, we met a Salvage Company at work. They told us that we were the first people they had seen since they had been there, and they laughed at our mission. That warren of trenches and dug-outs extended for untold miles, and we might as well look for a needle in a haystack. They warned us, if we insisted on going further in, not to let any man go singly, but only in strong parties, as the Golgotha was peopled with wild men, British, French, Australian, German deserters, who lived there underground, like ghouls among the mouldering dead, and who came out at nights to plunder and kill.
>
> In the night, an officer said, mingled with the snarling of the carrion dogs, they often heard inhuman cries and rifle shots coming from that awful wilderness, as though the bestial denizens were fighting amongst themselves; and none of the Salvage Company ever ventured beyond the confines of their camp after the sun had set. Once they had put out, as a trap, a basket containing food, tobacco and a bottle of whisky. But the following morning they found the bait untouched, and a note in the basket: 'Nothing doing!' We proceeded on our way very much interested in this queer story.

The myth of the wild deserters continued to strike a chord long after the end of the war, and in 1985 formed the basis of the novel *No Man's Land*, by Reginald Hill. The theme was also woven into the fabric of the acclaimed Australian television war drama, *Anzacs*.

The use of Golgotha as a metaphor for the searing brutality of war, and of the enemy, reached its apex in the myth of the Crucified Canadian. In the middle of May 1915, just weeks after the first use of poison gas by the Germans at Ypres, and coinciding neatly with the sinking of the *Lusitania* and the Bryce Report, the Allied press became briefly preoccupied with a gruesome atrocity story which had already gained wide currency at the Front. In a new twist to an existing myth concerning atrocities against Belgian civilians, it was said that in April a Canadian soldier had been found crucified near Ypres. The charge of crucifixion served to underline the ruthless actions of a Godless foe who would stop at nothing, not even the most painful form of killing devised in 2,000 years. The popularity of the Canadian story also coincided with the resurrection of *The Bowmen* at Mons as an angelic host, and the arrival of the Christ-like Comrade in White on the battlefields of Flanders and France.

In fact the allegation was not new. Suggestions that a British officer had been crucified and set alight near Le Cateau in September 1914 were already in circulation, while Ian Hay had offered a circumstantial description of the crucifixion of a wounded British soldier by Uhlans in the *First Hundred Thousand*, his popular but semi-fictionalized tribute to Kitchener's New Armies. Neither story made much headway, however, and both were probably disbelieved, or else lost in the deluge of similar atrocity stories which flooded back across the Channel during the first months of the war. The fact that the alleged crucifixion of a Canadian soldier in April 1915 immediately became headline news around the world stands as compelling evidence that it was actively promoted – and probably invented – by official sources as a military counterpart to the *Lusitania* tragedy. The first report to appear in the British press was run by *The Times* on May 10th:

Last week a large number of Canadian soldiers wounded in the fighting round Ypres arrived at the base hospital at Versailles.

They all told the story of how one of their officers had been crucified by the Germans. He had been pinned to a wall by bayonets thrust through his hands and feet, another bayonet had then been driven through his throat, and, finally, he was riddled with bullets. The wounded Canadians said that the Dublin Fusiliers had seen this done with their own eyes, and that they had heard the officers of the Dublin Fusiliers talking about it.

The following day the *Toronto Star* published a front page report beneath the byline Windermere, which told of a Canadian sergeant clamped to a tree by his arms and legs, and bayoneted 60 times. The story, said to have provoked a 'great, sullen anger' amongst the soldiery, came second-hand from a witness who had died in the arms of a Red Cross volunteer:

C.J.C. Clayton, a New Zealander, who is serving with the British Red Cross and is now wounded, brings a message from Captain R.A.S. Allen of the fifth Canadian Battalion, who comes from Vancouver, and who died of wounds in a hospital in Boulogne May 2, confirming the horrible story of the crucifixion of a Canadian sergeant by the Germans. Clayton says . . .

'Allen went on to declare that he and a medical officer, major, and others all signed a sworn statement attesting the truth of a detailed record of the crucifixion. A Canadian sergeant was tied up by the arms and legs to a tree and pierced sixty times by German bayonets.'

Clayton says the sergeant's name was given him by Allen, but in the confusion of wounding he cannot now find it . . .

The same *Star* dispatch also carried a paragraph from the Paris correspondent of the *Morning Post*, which reported a rumour current among Canadian soldiers about a sergeant who had been crucified with bayonets, this time to a door:

Wounded Canadians here are all certain that the enemy is particularly vindictive towards them, as the Germans have been furious that the Canadians did not stay in Canada instead of coming over to help England. The Canadians are all firmly of the belief that a Canadian soldier was crucified. They assert they heard it from officers in the Dublin Fusiliers who actually came across the body nailed to a door with hands and feet pierced with bayonets. The body was riddled with bullets.

The same correspondent says Canadians who now come to Paris hospitals after the Ypres fighting are extremely taciturn about their share in it.

This latest atrocity story prompted yet another public outcry, replete with minor rioting in London, and several questions in the Commons. On May 12th an MP called Houston asked the long-suffering Under Secretary of State for War, Harold Tennant, whether he had:

Any information regarding the crucifixion of three Canadian soldiers recently captured by the Germans, who nailed them with bayonets to the side of a wooden structure.

By way of reply, Houston was informed that no eyewitness reports had been received, but that inquiries would be made. Meanwhile the story grew quickly in the telling. On the same day, May 12th, the Reverend Clark recorded in his rural parish of Great Leighs in Essex:

James Caldwell said he had just come from London and has seen there personally an invalided officer of the Canadians. This officer told him that the report about the 'crucifying' of Canadians was true. He had himself seen one of his men who was nailed by bayonets on to wooden boards. Of 2,000 men, only 220 in his division were now fully fit for duty owing to the poisoned gas . . .

Mr Caldwell said that there were this afternoon great tumults in the East End of London. The people are stung to fury partly by the *Lusitania* murders, but still more by the torture of the Canadians. Everywhere they have been attacking Germans and German shops. One result of the Lusitanian and Canadian sufferings has been a tremendous rush of recruits.

That the tale of the Crucified Canadian provided a boost both to recruitment and the Allied cause generally is borne out by the American writer Dalton Trumbo, who recorded:

> The Los Angeles newspapers carried a story of two young Canadian soldiers who had been crucified by the Germans in full view of their comrades across No Man's Land. That made the Germans nothing better than animals, and naturally you got interested and wanted Germany to get the tar kicked out of her.

A flurry of letters were said to have been received in Canada from the Front. On the 14th a Canadian private wrote home to his wife that not one but six of his comrades had been crucified, and their bodies adorned with a notice warning all other Canadians 'to stop in Canada'. Another private was told that after a section of Allied trench had been retaken, a Canadian soldier was found with large nails driven through the palms of his hands. The next time this particular unit was in combat, so it was said, the officers ordered that no German prisoners should be taken. Some versions claimed that the unit concerned was a battalion from Toronto area; others that the location was St Julien, north-east of Ypres, or else Maple Copse near Sanctuary Wood, to the south.

Further details also appeared in the papers, with both the tree and the door now replaced by a fence. On May 15th a *Times* correspondent in France reported on what was now described as an 'insensate act of hate':

> The story . . . of the crucifixion of a Canadian officer during the fighting at Ypres on April 22–23 is in substance true. The story was current here at the time, but, in the absence of direct evidence and absolute proof, men were unwilling to believe that a civilized foe could be guilty of an act so cruel and savage. Now, I have reason to believe, written depositions testifying to the fact of the discovery of the body are in possession of the British Headquarter Staff.
>
> The unfortunate victim was a sergeant. As the story was told to me, he was found transfixed to the wooden fence of a farm

building. Bayonets were thrust through the palms of his hands and feet, pinning him to the fence. He had been repeatedly stabbed with bayonets, and there were many punctured wounds in his body.

I have not heard that any of our men actually saw the crime committed. There is room for the supposition that the man was dead before he was pinned to the fence, and that the enemy in his insensate rage and hate of the English wreaked his vengeance on the lifeless body of his foe. That is the most charitable complexion that can be put upon the deed, ghastly as it is.

There is not a man in the ranks of the Canadians who fought at Ypres who is not firmly convinced that this vile thing has been done. They know, too, that the enemy bayonetted their wounded and helpless comrades in the trenches.

On the same day the *Plymouth Evening Herald* ran a report which claimed that one Trooper Needs of the 2nd Life Guards (machine gun section) had written home to a friend:

The Canadians fought grandly, and completely routed the enemy, capturing all they had lost and more besides. As they advanced they found two of their comrades nailed to doors, quite dead. I wonder what Dr Lyttleton will think of that. I expect he will say 'Be kind to the Germans.' Yes, and like one of the Canadian officers said, I guess, sonny, we will.

In the House of Commons on the 19th, Houston against asked whether Tennant had access to any official information:

Showing that during the recent fighting, when the Canadians were temporarily driven back, they were compelled to leave about 40 of their wounded comrades in a barn, and then on recapturing their position found the Germans had bayoneted all the wounded with the exception of a sergeant, and that the Germans had removed the figure of Christ from the large village crucifix and fastened the sergeant while alive on the cross; and whether he is aware that the crucifixion of our soldiers is becoming a practice of the Germans?

Tennant replied that no such story had been confirmed, although enquiries were not yet complete. These included an investigation by the Canadian Judge Advocate General's office, as reported by Canon Frederick Scott, the well-known Canadian army chaplain, in his 1922 memoir *The Great War as I Saw It*. Recording a meeting with the Deputy Judge Advocate General at Bailleul in late May or early June 1915:

> He . . . told me of his business. There had been a report that one of our Highlanders had been crucified on the door of a barn. The Roman Catholic chaplain of the 3rd Brigade and myself had tried to trace the story to its origin. We found that the nearest we could get to it was, someone had told somebody else about it. One day I managed to discover a Canadian soldier who said he had seen the crucifixion himself. I at once took some paper out of my pocket and a New Testament and told him, 'I want you to make that statement on oath and put your signature to it.' He said, 'It is not necessary.' But he had been talking so much about the matter to the men around him that he could not escape.
>
> I had kept his sworn testimony in my pocket and it was to obtain this that the Deputy Judge Advocate General had called upon me. I gave it to him and told him that in spite of the oath, I thought the man was not telling the truth. Weeks afterwards I got a letter from the Deputy Judge telling me that he had found the man, who, when confronted by a Staff officer, weakened, and said he was mistaken in swearing that he had seen the crucifixion, he had only been told about it by somebody else.
>
> We have no right to charge the Germans with the crime. They have done so many things equally bad, that we do not need to bring charges against them of which we are not quite sure.

One sergeant? Two sergeants? Six? Nailed to a tree, a door, a fence or a cross? Inevitably the story was never verified by an official source, although in his memoir *At GHQ* Brigadier-General Charteris offers his own unreliable slant:

> The story . . . began in a report sent by a sergeant that he had seen Germans sitting round a lighted fire, and what looked like a crucified man. He worked his way closer to them, and found that it was only shadows cast by some crossed sticks on other objects. The report was transmitted back without this explanation.

The legend of the crucified soldier never quite faded, and found its way into several celebrated memoirs, including *Goodbye to All That* by Robert Graves (1929) and *Testament of Youth* by Vera Brittain (1933), as well as a poem, 'Jean Desprez', by the popular Scots/Canadian poet Robert Service, published in 1916. Another poet, Rudyard Kipling, was also convinced of the truth of the story. The myth was also tailored for different Allied uniforms in different locations. In 1915 Ian Hay had written that the victim was a wounded British soldier, crucified on a tree by Uhlans. In October of the same year, the Reverend Clark recorded another visit from his acquaintance James Caldwell, who was evidently preoccupied with the story:

> He told me that the Argyll and Sutherland Highlanders had found two of their men crucified, nailed to a tree. Since then they have naturally been in a fury, and it has been bayonet not quarter for the Germans. Their wrath is well known among the other regiments who amuse themselves by inventing grim stories to set it forth.

A lurid American propaganda film from 1918, *The Prussian Cur*, written and directed by Raoul Walsh, recreated the crucifixion scene in graphic detail, together with the sinking of the *Lusitania*. A later American variation on the basic crucifixion story printed in the *Pittsburgh Sunday Post* in February 1919 proved equally fictitious. By this account, a detachment of the Fifth Marines entering the village of Suippes the previous October found a naked girl nailed to a barn door, and half the coffins in the churchyard 'torn from the graves' and opened, apparently with the idea of despoiling corpses. Yet despite prompt denials both from Washington and from a Catholic clergyman in Suippes, the story was later adapted as the basis of a war propaganda drama by Francis Nielson, titled *Duty to Civilization*.

   The myth of the Crucified Canadian lived on in *Canada's Golgotha* (Plate 26), a bas-relief frieze sculpted in bronze by a British artist, Francis Derwent Wood (1871–1926), whose other works include the Machine Gun Corps memorial at Hyde Park Corner. The piece showed mocking German soldiers beneath the crucifix, taunting the dying man's agony, and was first exhibited as part of the Canadian War Memorials Exhibition in London in January 1919. The German government immediately protested that the accusation of crucifixion by its army amounted to libel, and demanded the production of evidence. By April, two sworn statements had been obtained from Allied soldiers who claimed to provide eyewitness accounts. Leonard Vivian, a former bandsman and stretcher-bearer with the Middlesex Regiment, gave the location as a barn between the front line and his dressing station just outside the village of St Julien, north-east of Ypres, and the date as April 23rd 1915:

> I saw on the right hand side of the road on a barn door what appeared to me to be a Canadian sergeant crucified to the door. There was a bayonet through each hand and his head was hanging forward as though he were dead or unconscious . . . I learned from Canadians the same day that this sergeant was a Canadian and had been crucified for protecting an old woman . . . This sergeant did not wear kilts, or if he did, he had an overcoat over them.

The second deposition was provided by William Metcalfe, a Canadian corporal who had been transferred to 'No 2 platoon of the 16th Canadian Battalion' on or about April 21st. At the time his statement was sworn, Metcalfe – a recipient of both the Victoria Cross and the Military Medal – was a patient at the Cooden Hospital in Sussex. By his account:

My platoon was proceeding along the St Jean road when I noticed
a soldier pinned to a barn door with bayonets. The barn door was
on the left hand side of the road going up. There was a bayonet
through each wrist. His head hung forward on his breast as
though he were dead. I could not see any bullet wound but did
notice Maple Leaf badges on his collar. We were told later that this
man belonged to the 16th Battalion but I saw no badges other
than those I have mentioned to vouchsafe this. He had no
headdress on when I saw him. The platoon sergeant, whose name
I cannot remember, examined the body and we moved on.

St Julien and St Jean are neighbouring villages, and in April 1915
were the scene of fierce fighting, during which the opposing lines
fluctuated, and which resulted in the capture of St Julien by the
Germans on April 24th. It is impossible to test the reliability of either
statement. Both seem to have been hurriedly obtained, and relate to
locations some two miles apart. Moreover, these descriptions of the
crucified man seem remarkably close to the sculpture by Derwent
Wood. Even in the midst of the fierce and fluid battle, it seems odd
that the corpse was left nailed to the door, despite the fact that a
large number of troops passed by, and had time to inspect it.
Nevertheless, the evidence was sufficient for the Colonial Office in
London, who informed Berlin via a Swiss mediator:

> Included in the evidence so far in the possession of the Canadian
> government are sworn statements by soldiers of the best character
> serving both with the Canadian and Imperial Forces who were
> unknown to one another, and between whom there was no
> possibility of collusion.

But in Canada a greater degree of scepticism prevailed. In 1919 a
paper called the *Nation* published a letter from Private Loader of the
2nd Battalion of the Royal West Kent Regiment, who claimed to
have seen the crucified man with his own eyes. However, in a
subsequent letter the paper was informed by Captain E.N. Bennett
that no such private had ever served with the regiment, and that the

2nd Battalion had been in India throughout the conflict. Nor would it seem that the version given by Harold Peat, alleging the crucifixion of three Canadian sergeants near St Julien, was treated seriously.

Meanwhile several senior establishment figures in Canada denounced the story as false. Ernest Chambers, the wartime press censor, concluded that the story had been invented in America with the object of boosting recruitment. Lieutenant-General Sir Arthur Currie, the commander of the Canadian Corps on the Western Front from 1917 onwards, also found it was a fabrication. Following German protests over the exhibition of the Wood sculpture in 1919, a Canadian officer named Richardson was dispatched to Europe in an attempt to authenticate the outrage, but the only first-hand statement obtained cast a very different light on the incident. According to Major G.C. Carvell, formerly of the Princess Patricia's Canadian Light Infantry, the victim had been killed by Belgian farmers:

The 'crucifixion' was not one IN FACT. [He] had been tied up by wire attached to his wrists and feet, while a strand, which held his head in position against the wall, accounted for his semi-strangulation.

According to Carvell, the incident had taken place 'on an afternoon in April 1915' at least 11,000 yards away from the nearest German troops. By this stage, August 1919, the whole affair had become a political embarrassment between Ottawa, London and Berlin, and the investigation did not proceed further. In June 1920 the Canadian War Memorials Exhibition withdrew the controversial sculpture, with the result that *Canada's Golgotha* was lost to public view until 1988.

As with the celebrated 'man who never was' who later served the Allies so well in 1943, periodic attempts have been made to identify the Crucified Canadian. In April 2001 the *Sunday Express* published an article by journalist Iain Overton which claimed that a Canadian sergeant was crucified near Ypres on April 24th 1915, and identified

1 Carl Lody in the dock during his trial at the Middlesex Guildhall in October 1914. Lody was shot in the Tower of London in November, having contributed both to spy mania and the myth of Russians in England.

2 The spy mania of 1914 produced a scare that the reverse of enamelled signs for Maggi soup carried messages for enemy agents.

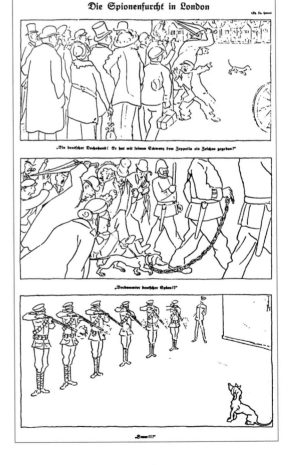

3 Spy terror in London, November 1914. From top to bottom: a boy points out a dachsund, warning that it has signalled to a Zeppelin with its tail; the outraged crowd execrates the 'damned German spy', which is led away by the police; the unfortunate dog is executed by firing squad.

IS **YOUR** HOME WORTH FIGHTING FOR?

IT WILL BE TOO LATE TO FIGHT WHEN THE ENEMY IS AT YOUR DOOR

SO **JOIN TO-DAY**

able.

THE RUSSIANS.

Official Denial that they are in France or Belgium.

The Press Bureau issued the following last night:

There is no truth whatever in the rumours that Russian soldiers have landed in, or passed through, Great Britain on their way to France or Belgium.

The statements that Russian troops are now on Belgian or French soil should be discredited.

4 *Left*: The invasion scare is exploited to boost army recruitment in this 'Join Today' poster.
5 *Above*: Official denial of the presence of Russians in England, issued 15 September 1914. (*Daily News and Leader*)

6 Enemy saboteurs and an invisible Zeppelin were among the mythical culprits blamed for the widespread destruction caused by the explosion at Silvertown in January 1917. Ruined terraced houses in Fort Street. (*East Ham Public Libraries*)

How a detachment of the Royal Marine Light Infantry marched out of a railway station after detraining on the Continent in 1914.—(*Daily Sketch*.)

7 Arrival of the Royal Marine Brigade in Antwerp. It was hoped that German spies might mistake the Marines for Russian reinforcements. (*The Daily Sketch, 28 August 1914*)

8 Germany tried to counter Allied propaganda on alleged atrocities in Belgium and France with images such as this, but with little success. (*Courtesy Deborah Lake*)

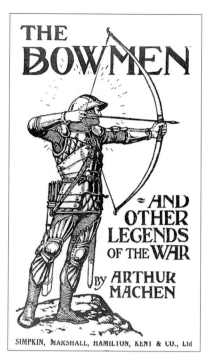

9 *Above*: Cover of the 1915 book edition of Arthur Machen's short story 'The Bowmen' (*Courtesy Neil R. Storey*)

10 *Right*: Contemporary illustration of bowmen assisting the BEF during the Retreat from Mons.

11 Alfred Pearse's illustration of the Angel of Mons from *The Chariots of God*, 1931. Here the 'angels' take the form of protecting spirits. (*Mary Evans Picture Library*)

12 An overtly religious interpretation of the Comrade in White, or white helper.

Atrocity or legitimate act? While the cartoon from 1914 in effect depicts the murder of a child (**13**), a contemporary photograph from Belgium clearly shows a scout equipped with a Lee Enfield rifle, as well as other items of British military equipment (**14**). (*Photograph courtesy Deborah Lake*)

THE HUNS CAPTURED SOME OF OUR FISHERMEN IN THE NORTH SEA AND TOOK THEM TO SENNELAGER. THEY CHARGED THEM WITHOUT A SHRED OF EVIDENCE WITH BEING "MINE LAYERS". THEY ORDERED THEM TO BE PUNISHED WITHOUT A TRIAL. THAT PUNISHMENT CONSISTED IN SHAVING ALL THE HAIR OFF ONE SIDE OF THE HEAD AND FACE. THE HUNS THEN MARCHED THEIR VICTIMS THROUGH THE STREETS AND EXPOSED THEM TO THE JEERS OF THE GERMAN POPULACE.

BRITISH SAILORS! LOOK! READ! AND REMEMBER!

15 A depiction of so-called 'Hun' atrocity against civilians in Belgium. The amputation of hands and breasts was a favourite theme.

16 Poster showing alleged indignities suffered by British prisoners-of-war.

THE ROAD TO GLORY

17 The spitting of babies on bayonets was a popular atrocity story, as was the notion that the German army was exclusively comprised of drunken looters.

18 Recruitment to the colours is clearly the object of this British advertisement from 1915.

19 Cartoonist Louis Raemaekers'
grisly image of leaking body fats
illustrates the German 'corpse
factory' myth. (*Punch, 1917*)

Alas! My poor Brother!

20 A variant on the corpse factory
theme by Captain Bruce
Bairnsfather. The cartoon originally
appeared in *The Bystander*.

CANNON-FODDER—AND AFTER.

KAISER (*to 1917 Recruit*). "AND DON'T FORGET THAT YOUR KAISER WILL FIND A USE FOR YOU—ALIVE OR DEAD."

[At the enemy's "Establishment for the Utilisation of Corpses" the dead bodies of German soldiers are treated chemically the chief commercial products being lubricant oils and pigs' food.]

21 The Kaiser warns a recruit that '. . . your Kaiser will find a use for you – alive or dead.' The corpse factory can be seen below the balcony. (*Punch, April 1917*)

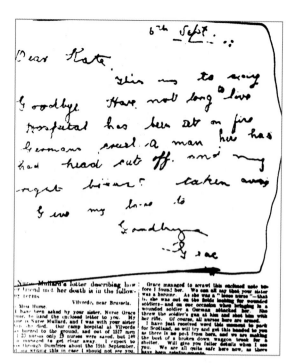

6th Sept.

Dear Kate,

this is to say goodbye. Have not long to live hospital has been set on fire germans crncl a man here has had head cut off. and my right bieas? taken away I see my love to Goodbye

22 The 'last note' of the murdered nurse Grace Hume, an atrocity story quickly exposed as false by *The Times* in September 1914.

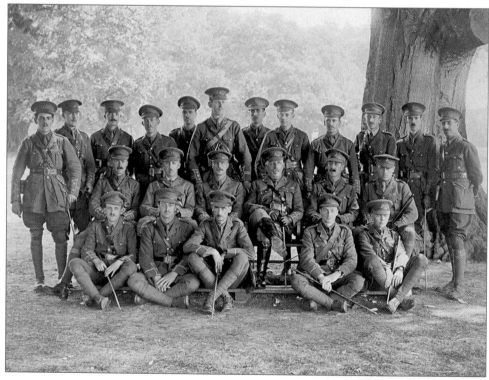

23 Officers of the 1/5th (Territorial) Battalion of the Norfolk Regiment, 1914: centre, Lieutenant-Colonel Horace Proctor-Beauchamp; far right, Captain Frank Beck. (*Courtesy Neil R. Storey*)

24 Field Marshal Sir Douglas Haig. The depiction of all British Great War generals as butchers and bunglers is one of the most damaging myths to emerge from the conflict. (*Courtesy Neil R. Storey*)

25 Lord Kitchener's death in June 1916 gave rise to several bizarre rumours. Some blamed his death on the mythical Hidden Hand. (*Courtesy Neil R. Storey*)

26 *Canada's Golgotha* by Francis Derwent-Wood, was first exhibited at the Royal Academy in London in 1919, but withdrawn from public view by the Canadian government in 1920. Official investigations were unable to confirm that a Canadian sergeant was crucified near Ypres in April 1915. (© *Canadian War Museum*)

LEUR " KULTUR "

Septembre 1914. — Dans un village près du Cateau, les Anglais trouvèrent
en le réoccupant, un officier anglais crucifié et à moitié brûlé. Cet épouvan-
table forfait fut vengé.

La Liberté, 24 Septembre 1914 :

27 Reports of the crucifixion of soldiers and civilians first appeared in 1914. This cartoon describes the reoccupation of a village near Le Cateau, where a British officer has been crucified and set alight. (*I.E. Paris, September 1914*)

28 Crucifixion scene from *The Prussian Cur*, an American silent picture written and directed by Raoul Walsh in 1918.

29 Noel Pemberton-Billing, Independent MP for East Hertfordshire, on the campaign trail in March 1916. The car was no less extravagant than his claims regarding the threat posed by the Hidden Hand. (*Associated Newspapers*)

30 American-born dancer Maud Allan in the role of Salome, April 1918. (*Mander and Mitchenson Theatre Collection*)

the man as Harry Band of the 48th Canadian Highlanders. According to research by Overton, in April 1915:

A Canadian soldier called George Barrie was detached from his regiment and had sought refuge from a gas attack in the village of St Julien, in Belgium. He lay rigid in a ditch as a group of German soldiers milled around a shed 50 yards away. When they left under cover of darkness, Barrie made his way over to where they had been.

Through the gloom, he saw a man in a British uniform, apparently leaning against a door. He called out and, when there was no reply, he edged closer. The sight that greeted his eyes was horrifying. A young sergeant was suspended 18 inches from the ground, pinned by eight bayonets which had been thrust through his limbs and torso. He had been crucified.

Band, a Scot born in Montrose in 1885, is said to have been reported missing, presumed dead, on April 24th. He has no known grave, although his descendants in British Columbia spoke of dark hints given when news of his death reached home. The honour roll of the Ontario Temperance Society, of which Band was a member, lists him as having 'met death by crucifixion while in the hands of the enemy', but this roll was not prepared until the 1930s. A note associated with the Wood sculpture suggests Band was the soldier in question, but again is a later addition. At first glance, the date and location tally loosely with the account published in *The Times* on May 15th, and with the sworn statements provided by Metcalfe and Vivien in 1919, but problems remain. The records of the Commonwealth War Graves Commission indicate that the only Canadian soldier named Band who died in 1915 was a private in the 16th Battalion, not the 48th Highlanders. Although this Private Band was indeed killed on April 24th, while serving in the same battalion as William Metcalfe and fighting in the same action, these several inconsistencies go a long way towards explaining why the fate of a named soldier was not exploited with more precision in 1915, or indeed why a string of official enquiries over the next four years were unable to substantiate the story.

The legend of the German corpse rendering factory remains the most notorious atrocity myth of the conflict, and fully deserves its appraisal by George Viereck as 'the master hoax' of the First World War. Indeed the story proved so durable that it would not finally be exposed as a fiction until 1925. The central premise of this ghoulish tale, first circulated in its popular form in April 1917, was that close behind their front line the Germans had established a facility for boiling down the corpses of dead soldiers, the by-products being used in the production of munitions, soap, fertiliser and pig food. For the Allied propaganda machine, the story played as a near-perfect conjunction of German science and Hunnish barbarity. Today, credit for the deliberate creation of the myth is usually given to British intelligence agencies, and in particular the omnipresent General Charteris. Yet this is itself a falsehood, for rumours of the existence of a German corpse factory were noted long before April 1917. For example, in a unique diary entry for June 16th 1915 the Prime Minister's daughter-in-law, Cynthia Asquith, records a flippant discussion on the subject:

> Quite a pleasant dinner. We discussed the rumour that the Germans utilise even their corpses by converting them into glycerine with the by-product of soap. I suggested that Haldane should offer his vast body as raw material to Lloyd George. We played poker after dinner. I played in a syndicate with Papa [Herbert Asquith], which is always unsatisfactory. The syndicate lost about a pound.

Almost a century later it is impossible to say how the story first originated. Official British sources have repeatedly claimed that the story first appeared in the pages of an obscure Belgian newspaper printed in France, *Indépendence Belge*, on April 10th, which was itself extracted from an earlier edition of the journal *La Belgique*, published at Leyden in Holland. This, too, is untrue, as we shall see. Nevertheless, the original report from April 1917, which reads like a nightmarish parody of Jules Verne or H.G. Wells, merits quotation at length, for it was diligently constructed by its author, with particular attention paid to precise scientific and technological detail:

We have known for long that the Germans stripped their dead behind the firing line, fastened them into bundles of three or four bodies with iron wire, and then dispatched these grisly bundles to the rear. Until recently the trains laden with the dead were sent to Seraing, near Liège, and to a point north of Brussels, where there were refuse consumers. Much surprise was caused by the fact that of late this traffic has proceeded in the direction of Gerolstein, and it is noted that on each wagon was written DAVG.

German science is responsible for the ghoulish idea of the formation of the German Offal Utilization Company Limited (DAVG), a dividend-earning company with a capital of £250,000, the chief factory of which has been constructed 1,000 yards from the railway connecting St Vith, near the Belgian frontier, with Gerolstein, in the lonely, little-frequented Eifel district, south-west of Coblenz. The factory deals specially with the dead from the West Front. If the results are as good as the company hopes, another will be established to deal with corpses on the East Front.

The factory is invisible from the railway. It is placed deep in forest country, with a specially thick growth of trees about it. Live wires surround it. A special double track leads up to it. The works are about 700 feet long and 110 feet broad, and the railway runs completely round them. In the north-west corner of the works the discharge of the trains takes place.

The trains arrive full of bare bodies, which are unloaded by the workers who live at the works. The men wear oilskin overalls and masks with mica eyepieces. They are equipped with long hooked poles, and push the bundles of bodies to an endless chain, which picks them with big hooks, attached at intervals of two feet. The bodies are transported on this endless chain into a long, narrow compartment, where they pass through a bath which disinfects them. They then go through a drying chamber, and finally are automatically carried into a digester or great cauldron, in which they are dropped by an apparatus which detaches them from the chain. In the digester they remain for six to eight hours, and are treated by steam, which breaks them up while they are slowly stirred by machinery.

From this treatment result several products. The fats are broken up into stearine, a form of tallow, and oils, which require to be re-distilled before they can be used. The process of distillation is carried out by boiling the oil with carbonate of soda, and some part of the by-products resulting from this is used by German soap makers. The oil distillery and refinery lie in the south-eastern corner of the works. The refined oil is sent out in small casks like those used for petroleum, and is of a yellowish brown colour.

The fumes are exhausted from the buildings by electric fans, and are sucked through a great pipe to the north-eastern corner, where they are condensed and the refuse resulting is discharged into a sewer. There is no high chimney, as the boiler furnaces are supplied with air by electric fans. There is a laboratory and in charge of the works is a chief chemist with two assistants and 78 men. All the employees are soldiers and are attached to the 8th Army Corps. There is a sanatorium by the works, and under no pretext is any man permitted to leave them. They are guarded as prisoners at their appalling work.

Within days other fragments were revealed. On the 16th *The Times* ran a short piece translated from the a Berlin newspaper, the *Lokalanzeiger*, written by Karl Rosner, its special correspondent on the Western Front. This too had originally appeared on April 10th:

We pass through Everingcourt. There is a dull smell in the air, as if lime were being burnt. We are passing the great Corpse Exploitation Establishment (Kadaververwertungsanstalt) of this Army Group. The fat that is won here is turned into lubricating oils, and everything else is ground down in the bones mill into a powder, which is used for mixing with pigs' food and as manure. Nothing can be permitted to go to waste.

The Times added, by way of corroboration:

It will be remembered that one of the American Consuls, on leaving Germany in February, stated in Switzerland that the

Germans were distilling glycerine for nitro-glycerine from the bodies of their dead, and thus were obtaining some part of their explosives.

The following day *The Times* ran the longer descriptive piece said to have appeared in the *Indépendence Belge*, albeit 'omitting some of the most repulsive details', and from this point on the story snowballed rapidly. One reader suggested the story should be spread in neutral countries and the east, where it would be likely to horrify Buddhists, Hindus and Mohammedans. Other correspondents questioned the translation of the German word *Kadaver*, suggesting that it was not applicable to human corpses. The *Lancet* published an article in which certain technical aspects of the process were considered, it being calculated that 1,000 bodies at an average weight of 10 stones might yield about two tons of fat (on an average of 3 per cent basis of fat per body weight), which in turn could be converted into a tenth of this weight in glycerine. Elsewhere both the Chinese Ambassador and the Maharajah of Bikanir issued public expressions of horror at German treatment of the dead, the latter promising that if the bodies of Indian soldiers were exploited in like fashion, such an atrocity would never be forgotten or forgiven in India.

The story travelled quickly in America, and over the course of the next fortnight other accounts, held to be corroborative, entered into circulation. On April 20th *The Times* reported:

Among the stories told by men who have come from the front is the following, which affords unexpected confirmation of the account of the Corpse Utilization Company's enterprise. The soldier who tells the story is Sergeant B- of the Kents. Describing the prisoners taken in the recent fighting, he said:

One of them who spoke English told me – mind, I don't know that it's true, but he told me – that even when they're dead their work isn't done. They are wired together in batches then, and boiled down in factories as a business, to make fat for munition making and to feed pigs and poultry, and God knows what else besides. Then other folk eat the pigs and poultry, so you may say it's cannibalism, isn't it? This fellow told me Fritz calls his margarine 'corpse fat', because they suspect that's what it comes from.

The very next day, in its daily review of foreign press reports and intercepted letters, the Ministry of Information included one from the Hague which seemed to confirm several details contained in the original report from *La Belgique*. The letter told of a German freight car observed in a railway siding on the Dutch frontier, which became a focus of attention after it began to give off a vile smell. When opened, the wagon was found to be packed tight with dead soldiers, roped in bundles of four, stood on end and fully clothed. The car, the letter continued, had been diverted to Holland by mistake, and was supposed to be routed to Liège, where the Germans had established their corpse utilization plant. The story first appeared in a Belgian newspaper, whose editor had learned of the incident from a Belgian officer, and formed the basis of an unusually subtle (but still chilling) illustration by the celebrated Dutch cartoonist Louis Ramaekers.

The Germans protested loudly that such 'loathsome and ridiculous' reports were the result of deliberate mistranslation of the piece in the *Lokalanzeiger*, in which the word *Kadaver* referred only to animal remains, chiefly horses. In Britain, several sceptical MPs pressed the government for clarification, including the Irish member John Dillon and the member for Hanley, R.L. Outhwaite. On April 30th a heated exchange in the Commons included the following:

DILLON: Has their attention been turned to the fact that it is not only a gross scandal, but a very great evil to this country to allow the circulation of such statements, authorised by Ministers of the Crown, if they are, as I believe them to be, absolutely false?
OUTHWAITE: May I ask if the Noble Lord is aware that the circulation of these reports has caused anxiety and misery to British people who have lost their sons on the battlefield, and who think that their bodies may be put to this purpose, and does not that give a reason why he should try to find out the truth of what is happening in Germany?

The reply provided by Lord Robert Cecil, the Under Secretary for Foreign Affairs, appeared to lend substance to the original report without the responsibility of actually doing so:

LORD CECIL: In view of other actions by German military authorities there is nothing incredible in the present charge against them . . . I confess I am not able to attach very great importance to any statements made by the German government.

And so allegation and counter-allegation continued to fly back and forth between London and Berlin. *John Bull* and *Punch* printed mordant cartoons, while the *Daily Mail* published an article by a colonel which traced the Germans back to a wolf tribe who fed their corpses to dogs. The same piece reminded readers that German heroes ate corpses at their banquets in Valhalla. The poet Rudyard Kipling was inspired to pen a black parody of Thackeray's *Sorrow of Werther*, in which Charlotte spread her dead lover 'lightly on her bread'. The usually sceptical magazine *Truth* became convinced of the reality of the story after Welsh troops, storming the Messines Ridge, were reported to have discovered 'unsavoury German corpses done up in bundles of three'. On May 4th *The Times* reported that:

Among the prisoners captured in the recent fighting was a German army doctor, who seems to have talked very interestingly on the subject of the conversion of corpses . . . saying that it was an entirely natural thing to do to convert human bodies, but, of course, not horses, as these were too valuable for food purposes. Horses' bones only might be used. He was of the opinion that probably the censors did not permit the German people to know too much about it. The doctor was quite serious, and took a merely scientific and utilitarian view of it.

On May 11th, the German Foreign Secretary, Herr Zimmerman, firmly denied to the Reichstag that the bodies of German soldiers were being used in the production of fat stuffs, and threatened editors in neutral territories with libel proceedings if the story was circulated further:

> No reasonable person among our enemies can have been in any uncertainty about the fact that this has to do with the bodies of animals and not of human beings. The fact that the word 'cadavre' in French is used for human beings and animals has been exploited by our enemies. We have rectified this subtle misunderstanding, which, against its better knowledge, has been used by the enemy press to mislead public opinion. In neutral countries, in so far as there is a tangible slanderous intention, criminal proceedings will be taken.

The source of the original story remains shrouded in purposeful mystery. Although both *La Belgique* and *Indépendence Belge* existed in April 1917, a clearly British-originated report that Germany was 'extracting glycerine out of dead soldiers' for use in munitions appeared in an English-language newspaper in Shanghai, the *North China Herald*, as early as March 3rd. It is possible that the Belgian papers sourced the story there, but more likely that the copy came direct from London. Ironically, the Department of Information at Wellington House initially declined to circulate the story. Its director, C.F.G. Masterman, rightly doubted the likelihood of the German censor permitting the publication of the article in the *Lokalanzeiger* which admitted that human corpses were being used for this purpose, and feared the damaging propaganda boomerang of an exposed falsehood. However, at the Foreign Office a number of officials were inclined to believe it. In an official minute dated 26 April 1917 the Foreign Secretary, Arthur Balfour, acknowledged that the documentary evidence was inconclusive, but added:

> While it should not be desirable that His Majesty's Government should take any responsibility as regards the story pending the receipt of further information, there does not, in view of the many atrocious actions of which the Germans have been guilty, appear to be any reason why it should not be true.

The relevant Foreign Office file lodged at the Public Record Office also reveals that R. McCleod, MP, claimed to have received a letter from a senior British officer serving in France. According to Brigadier Morrison, the Germans had been observed removing bodies from the vicinity of Vimy Ridge, where German graves were conspicuous by their absence. From there, so it was said, the corpses were transported to the notorious *Kadaver* factory. In consequence, Wellington House was instructed to proceed with the preparation of pamphlets in Portuguese, Spanish, Swedish and Dutch. A four-page pamphlet entitled *A Corpse-Conversion Factory* was also published in London. Despite this, Masterman continued to maintain after the war that the Department of Information had rejected the story.

In his authoritative book *The Great War and Modern Memory*, Paul Fussell notes an analogous legend concerning a fictional Reducer (or Destructor) constructed by the British at Etaples, although the story is probably an echo of the *Kadaveranstalt* myth. In 1924 the waters were muddied by the pacifist philosopher Bertrand Russell, in an essay on propaganda included in *These Eventful Years*, a war record published by the Encyclopaedia Britannica Company. By his account, the corpse factory story was released in China when that nation's participation in the war was desired, in the hope that it would shock the population:

> Worldwide publicity was given to the statement that the Germans boiled down human corpses in order to extract from them gelatine and other useful substances . . . The story was set going cynically by one of the employees in the British propaganda department, a man with a good knowledge of German, perfectly aware that 'Kadaver' means carcass not corpse, but aware also that, with the Allied command of the means of publicity, the misrepresentation could be made to 'go down.'

Russell did not identify his sources, and appears to have relied in part on inaccurate guesswork: the linguistic debate around the word *Kadaver* began only after the publication of the *Lokalanzeiger* article on April 10th, whereas the *North China Herald* piece had appeared more than a month earlier.

However, Russell was almost certainly correct in stating that the story was a deliberate British invention. Several sources identify a section of military intelligence as the author. In his autobiography, published in 1970, Ivor Montagu recalled that during the war his family were visited periodically by a favoured cousin, Major Hugh Pollard, then an intelligence officer

In the First World War . . . how we laughed at his cleverness when he told us how his department had launched the account of the German corpse factories and of how the Hun was using the myriads of trench-war casualties for making soap and margarine. He explained that he had originally thought up the idea himself to discredit the enemy among the populations of Oriental countries, hoping to play upon the respect for the dead that goes with ancestor-worship. To the surprise of the authorities it had caught on, and they were now making propaganda out of it everywhere. The tears ran down his cheeks as he told us of the story they had circulated of a consignment of soap from Germany arriving in Holland and being buried with full military honours. But, even for us, the taste of some of his tales began to grow sour after he became a Black and Tan.

Given that Montagu wrote his account a half-century after the fact, there is no way of knowing which elements were relayed by Major Pollard, and which the author may have subsequently absorbed from elsewhere. Besides which, by 1917 the very same rumour had been in limited circulation for two years, and had reached the ear of the Prime Minister, as the diary of Cynthia Asquith makes clear.

Probably the strangest twist in an already tangled tale came in 1925, when Brigadier-General John Charteris paid a visit to the United States. Charteris, by then the Conservative member for Dumfriesshire, gave a speech at a private dinner function at the National Arts Club, during the course of which he claimed responsibility for originating the canard of the corpse factory.

One day there came to the desk of General Charteris a mass of material taken from German prisoners and dead soldiers. In it were two pictures, one showing a train taking dead horses to the rear so that fat and other things needed for fertiliser and munitions might be obtained from them, and the other showing a train taking dead Germans to the rear for burial. On the picture showing the horses was the word 'cadaver' . . . General Charteris had the caption telling of 'cadaver' being sent back to the fat factory transposed to the picture showing the German dead, and had the photograph sent to a Chinese newspaper in Shanghai.

Like Pollard, Charteris was said to have selected an oriental outlet in full knowledge of the reverence in which the Chinese held their ancestors, and against a background of uncertainty of Chinese opinion towards the Germans. China had severed relations with Germany on March 13th 1917, but did not declare war until August. The ruse was undertaken in full expectation that the story would filter back to Europe and America. The report of his speech continued:

The controversy raged until all England thought it must be true, and the German newspapers printed indignant denials. The matter came up in the House of Commons and an interrogation was made which was referred to General Charteris, who answered that from what he knew of the German mentality, he was prepared for anything. It was the only time, he said, during the war when he actually dodged the truth.

The matter might have gone even further, for an ingenious person in his office offered to write a diary of a German soldier, telling of his transfer from the front after two years of fighting to an easy berth in a factory, and of his horror at finding that he was to assist there in boiling down his brother soldiers. He obtained a transfer to the front and was killed.

It was planned to place this forged diary in the clothing of a dead German soldier and have it discovered by a war correspondent who had a passion for German diaries. General Charteris decided that the deception had gone far enough and that there might be an error in the diary which would have led to the exposure of the falsity. Such a result would have imperilled all the British propaganda, he said, and he did not think it worth while, but the diary is now in the war museum in London.

The *New York Times* went on to report that Charteris entertained his audience with many stories of spies, and closed with an appeal to Americans to give England their sympathy during the then-current economic crisis. However these disclosures appear to have landed Charteris in hot water back in London, for on his return from the States at the beginning of November the former Chief of Intelligence was summoned to Whitehall by Sir Laming Worthington-Evans, the Secretary of State for War. Precisely what passed between the two men is unrecorded, although it seems likely that Charteris was reprimanded for revealing that the story was a deliberate falsehood. It is interesting to note that Charteris made no mention at all of the corpse factory in his memoir *At GHQ*, published in 1932, despite the fact that within it Charteris chose to pass comment (though seldom helpfully) on just about every other wartime myth and legend.

Charteris met the minister at the War Office on November 3rd, and left for Scotland later in the day. According to *The Times* on the 4th, upon his arrival in Glasgow Charteris issued the following statement:

On arrival in Scotland I was surprised to find that, in spite of the repudiation issued by me at New York through Reuter's Agency, some public interest was still excited in the entirely incorrect report of my remarks at a private dinner in New York. I feel it, therefore, necessary to give again a categorical denial to the statement attributed to me. Certain suggestions and speculations as regards the origin of the Kadaver story which have already been published in *Those Eventful Years* and elsewhere, which I repeated, are, doubtless unintentionally, but nevertheless unfortunately, turned into definite statements of fact and attributed to me.

Lest there should still be any doubt, let me say that I neither invented the Kadaver story, nor did I alter the captions in any photograph, nor did I use any faked material for propaganda purposes. The allegations that I did so are not only incorrect, but absurd; as propaganda was in no way under GHQ France, where I had charge of the intelligence services. I should be as interested as the general public to know what was the true origin of the Kadaver story. GHQ France only came in when the fictitious diary supporting the Kadaver story was submitted. When this diary was discovered to be fictitious it was at once rejected.

I have seen the Secretary of State [for War] this morning, and have explained the whole circumstances to him, and have his authority to say that he is perfectly satisfied.

It was also noted that the War Office now regarded the incident as closed, and that no further inquiry would be held. Therefore it will probably never be known whether the account given by Charteris in New York was truthful, but swiftly censored by London as too revealing, or whether the former intelligence chief had simply concocted an entertaining after-dinner story, not expecting that it would excite the interest of the press. Prior to his return from the States, Charteris told an American newsman that he had no intention of challenging the report in The *New York Times*, since any errors it might contain were only of minor importance – a statement which flatly contradicts what he later said in Glasgow. Indeed it is not even possible to confirm whether or not the forged diary was ever deposited at the Imperial War Museum. Researching the matter in 1975, author Phillip Knightley was able to establish only that the museum believed the diary was probably among a number of boxes of papers lodged there by military intelligence after the end of the war, but recalled soon afterwards.

Unsurprisingly, the hasty and inadequate denial issued by Charteris was not generally accepted. According to comment in *The Times* on the same day:

This paper makes the significant observation that in the course of his denial he offered no comment on his reported admission that he avoided telling the truth when questioned about the matter in the House of Commons, or on his own description of a scheme to support the Corpse Factory story by 'planting' a forged diary in the clothing of a dead German prisoner – a proposal which he only abandoned lest the deception might be discovered.

The matter was again raised in the House of Commons on November 24th 1925, this time by a Lieutenant-Commander Kenworthy. After Worthington-Evans rehearsed the reports carried by the *Lokalanzeiger*, *Indépendence Belge* and *La Belgique* on April 10th 1917, and re-stated that German dictionaries and anatomical works appeared to confirm that the word *Kadaver* could be used to mean human bodies, he confirmed that on the basis of the information available to the War Office in 1917, it had had no reason to doubt the truth of the story. But Kenworthy pressed on:

KENWORTHY: Does the Right Honourable Gentleman think it desirable, even now, to finally admit the inaccuracy of the original story, in view of Locarno and other things?
WORTHINGTON-EVANS: It is not a question of whether it was accurate or inaccurate. What I was concerned with was the information upon which the War Office acted at the time. Of course, the fact that there has been no corroboration since necessarily alters the complexion of the case, but I was dealing with the information in the possession of the authorities at the time.

None of which amounted to an unambiguous denial, which came finally from the Secretary of State for Foreign Affairs on December 2nd, in response to a question by Arthur Henderson, the Labour member for Burnley:

SIR AUSTEN CHAMBERLAIN: My Right Honourable Friend the Secretary of State for War told the House last week how the story reached His Majesty's Government in 1917. The Chancellor of the German Reich had authorised me to say, on the authority of the German government, that there was never any foundation for it. I need scarcely add that on behalf of His Majesty's Government I accept this denial, and I trust that this false report will not again be revived.

Perhaps the most telling comment on the whole inglorious episode was offered by an American editorial, from *The Times-Dispatch* of Richmond, Virginia for December 6th:

A few years ago the story of how the Kaiser was reducing human corpses to fat aroused the citizens of this and other enlightened nations to a fury of hatred. Normally sane men doubled their fists and rushed off to the nearest recruiting sergeant. Now they are being told, in effect, that they were dupes and fools; that their own officers deliberately goaded them to the desired boiling-point, using an infamous lie to arouse them, just as a grown bully whispers to one little boy that another little boy said he could lick him.

The encouraging sign found in this revolting admission of how modern war is waged is the natural inference that the modern man is not over-eager to throw himself at his brother's throat at the simple word of command. His passions must be played upon, so the propaganda bureau has taken its place as one of the chief weapons. In the next war, the propaganda must be more subtle and clever than the best the World War produced. These frank admissions of wholesale lying on the part of trusted Governments in the last war will not soon be forgotten.

C.E. Montague, a former infantry officer and the author of *Disenchantment*, had already expressed similar sentiments in 1922. His account of the discovery of a reputed *Kadaveranstalt* during the closing stages of the war reveals something of the extent to which trench myths such as the corpse factory and the Crucified Canadian were accepted as fact by many fighting troops:

Of all this kind of swordsmanship the most dashing feat was the circulation of the 'corpse factory' story. German troops, it was written in part of our Press, had got, in certain places near their front, a proper plant for boiling down the fat of their own dead. It was not said whether the product was to be used as a food, or as a lubricant or illuminant only. Chance brought me into one of the reputed seats of this refinement of frugality. It was on ground that our troops had just taken, in 1918.

At Bellicourt the St Quentin Canal goes into a long tunnel. Some little way in from its mouth you could find, with a flash-lamp, a small doorway cut in the tunnel's brick wall, on the tow-path side of the canal. The doorway led to the foot of a narrow staircase that wound up through the earth till it came to an end in a room about 20 feet long. It, too, was subterranean, but now its darkness was pierced by one sharp-edged shaft of sunlight let in through a neat round hole cut in the five or six feet of earth above.

Loaves, bits of meat, and articles of German equipment lay scattered about, and two big dixies or cauldrons, like those in which we stewed our tea, hung over two heaps of cold charcoal. Eight or ten bodies, lying pell-mell, nearly covered half the floor. They showed the usual effects of shell-fire. Another body, disembowelled and blown almost to rags, lay across one of the dixies and mixed with a puddle of coffee that it contained. A quite simple case. Shells had gone into cook-houses of ours, long before then, and had messed up the cooks with the stew.

An Australian sergeant, off duty and poking about, like a good Australian, for something to see, had come up the stairs too. He had heard the great fat-boiling yarn, and how this was the latest seat of the industry. Sadly he surveyed the disappointing scene. Ruefully he noted the hopelessly normal nature of all the proceedings that had produced it. Then he broke the silence in which we had made our several inspections.

'Can't believe a word you read, sir, can you?' he said with some bitterness. Life had failed to yield one of its advertised marvels. The press had lied again. The propagandist myth about Germans had cracked up once more. 'Can't believe a word you read' had long been becoming a kind of catch-phrase in the army. And now another good man had been duly confirmed in the faith, that whatever your pastors and masters tell you had best be assumed to be just a bellyfull of east wind.

Montague overstates his case, perhaps, but the point is well made.

CHAPTER SIX

Lions, Donkeys and Ironclads

In modern memory, the enduring popular stereotype of British infantry tactics in the First World War offers extended lines of hopelessly exposed troops floundering in a sea of mud, while attempting to cross No Man's Land beneath a hail of machine gun bullets, obstructed by barbed wire, and hindered rather than helped by the supporting artillery barrage. Their commanders, from 'Butcher' Haig downward, are portrayed as aloof, callous and incompetent figures, billeted in luxurious châteaux far behind the trenches in the front line, of which they knew nothing and cared less. General Ludendorff derided his enemy for pursuing strategic aims with little regard for tactical difficulties, and is said to have appraised the British army as 'lions led by donkeys'. In truth, this memorable phrase was applied to the British generals not by the German Deputy Chief of Staff, but by the historian Alan Clark in 1961, who in falsifying history in the interests of newsworthy copy did much to perpetuate the most facile yet damaging myth of the entire war.

In the years following the Armistice, and more particularly in the wake of the publication of the war memoirs of David Lloyd George, Field Marshal Sir Douglas Haig came to be widely vilified as the callous architect of a disastrous military strategy on the Western Front. His strategy was interpreted as one of attrition, in which the opposing armies were obliged to batter themselves to pieces, launching attack after attack regardless of cost. In particular the tragedy of the first day of the Somme offensive, on which the British army suffered record casualties of 57,000 men – fully one-half of the attacking force – has come to be seen as emblematic of the carnage and futility across the whole of the Western Front. That the actual number killed on that day was approximately 20,000 is less widely appreciated, as is that fact that the Somme campaign lasted a total of four and a half months, produced a lesser average of 2,500 casualties daily, played a significant part in the destruction of the German field army, and forced the BEF to develop tactics that would eventually win the war.

Nevertheless, the tragedy of July 1st 1916 has clouded perception ever since, and played a significant part in launching a veritable flotilla of myths. So too have the war poets – Sassoon, Owen, Graves, Blunden – a small and largely unrepresentative group of junior officers who are among the most quoted British voices from the First World War. Sassoon endorsed the popular perception of 'butchers and bunglers' as early as 1917 in his celebrated poem 'The General', thought to have been inspired by his then Corps commander, Lieutenant-General Sir Ivor Maxse:

> 'Good morning, good morning!' the General said
> When we met him last week on our way to the line.
> Now the soldiers he smiled at are most of 'em dead,
> And we're cursing his staff for incompetent swine.
> 'He's a cheery old card,' grunted Harry to Jack
> As they slogged up to Arras with rifle and pack.
> . . .
> But he did for them both by his plan of attack.

Few of his fellow poets were any kinder. Writing in 1936, eight years after the death of Haig, Lloyd George, the former Liberal Prime Minister, made plain his dislike of the same Generals collectively, and Haig in particular:

It is not too much to say that when the Great War broke out our Generals had the most important lessons of their art to learn.

Before they began they had much to unlearn. Their brains were cluttered with useless lumber . . . Some of it was never cleared out to the end of the War . . . They knew nothing except by hearsay about the actual fighting of a battle under modern conditions. Haig ordered too many bloody battles in this War. He only took part in two . . . He never even saw the ground on which his greatest battles were fought, either before or during the fight. . . . The distance between the châteaux and the dug-outs was as great as that from the fixed stars to the caverns of the earth.

Others subsequently carried their condemnation further still, the historian Basil Liddell Hart even suggesting that in the wake of 'manslaughter' on such an epic scale, those commanders responsible should be held accountable to the nation. Given that on one view the operational history of the British army on the Western Front between 1914 and mid-1918 constitutes a succession of *débâcles* and disasters, it is easy to contend that its heavy losses – half a million dead, one and a half million wounded – were entirely due to the ignorance and ineptitude of its commanders. But this, as we shall see, is no less a myth than the German corpse factory or the Angel of Mons.

In truth, the manner in which Haig and the General Staff conducted their war should be viewed in its proper context, and in particular bearing in mind the technology available at the time. The First World War was the first truly global conflict, and the first to involve technologies that are now taken for granted: aircraft, tanks, wireless telegraphy and chemical weapons. It was also the first great artillery war, and the first in which the machine gun achieved its full potential. It represented the first conflict of modern mass production, and widespread use of the internal combustion engine. As the historian John Terraine points out in his masterly study of wartime mythology, *The Smoke and the Fire*, the commanders on all sides found themselves caught in a hiatus of technology – and therefore of tactics – in which they were presented with the poisons well in advance of the antidote. Add to this the fact that Britain's small regular army had been effectively destroyed by early 1915, that the New Armies had to be trained and equipped almost from scratch, that the BEF was subordinated to French command throughout the conflict, and that too many major offensives were timed or launched for no better reason than to relieve pressure on its French and Russian allies, and it is little wonder that the First World War took four long years to win.

This is not to suggest that British strategy and tactics were never worthy of reproach, whether on the Somme or elsewhere. For example, on July 1st 1916 General Henry Rawlinson ordered his Fourth Army to cross No Man's Land in extended line at 'a steady pace', thus providing those German machine gunners not eliminated by the preceding artillery barrage with an exposed, slow-moving target. By no means all British troops advanced in this fashion, and therefore blame for the comparative slaughter on the left flank can hardly be credited to this factor alone. Indeed on the right flank the attackers succeeded in taking all their objectives, regardless of whether they advanced in extended line or skirmisher formation. Yet the myth of the slaughter by extended line persists, and dovetails with the misconception that British troops were too overloaded to move or fight properly. In the *Official History* by Sir James Edmonds, their slow and murderous progress across No Man's Land is falsely ascribed to the excessive weight of equipment carried by each soldier:

> The total weight carried per man was about 66 *lbs*, which made it difficult to get out of a trench, impossible to move much quicker than a slow walk, or to rise or lie down quickly . . . This overloading of men is by many infantry officers regarded as one of the principal reasons of the heavy losses and failure of their battalions; for their men could not get through the machine gun zone with sufficient speed.

While it is certainly true that a load equal to half a man's body weight greatly complicates the task of scrambling over the top of a trench, or rising from a prone position, it does not prevent him from moving forward at a jogtrot, or taking cover, nor would it utterly exhaust him in a mere matter of minutes. On the Somme, the distance between the opposing first line trenches was seldom greater than 500 yards, and the ground conditions reasonably firm and level in most sectors. Yet the myth perpetrated by Edmonds and Liddell Hart that 'hopelessly handicapped' troops found it 'physically impossible' to cross the machine gun zone to the German line at anything other than a snail's pace gained widespread acceptance, despite the fact that British troops were scarcely less heavily equipped in 1918, yet still managed to advance some 84 miles in 116 days.

But that is to leap forward in time. In truth, the tactical hiatus imposed by trench warfare was chiefly the result of new technologies rather than inept leadership. The preceding 60 years were marked by revolutionary increases in firepower, in particular the steady improvement of the rifle over the musket in terms of range, velocity and rate of fire. This in turn drastically reduced the effectiveness of horsed cavalry, the traditional arm of exploitation in a war of movement. As a result, trench warfare had already been encountered during previous campaigns, for example at Sebastopol (1854–55), Plevna (1877) and Port Arthur (1904–5). The development of the machine gun served only to seal the bargain. August and September 1914 produced a war of movement only because the Allied armies spent much of this period engaged in a fighting retreat. Once the German advance was checked at the Battle of the Marne, the digging of protective trenches along the Aisne became a foregone conclusion. The addition of barbed wire and increased numbers of automatic weapons served only to make the stalemate permanent. It would be two years before an all-new technical innovation capable of breaking what had become a form of siege warfare (the tank) rather than deepening it (artillery, poison gas) would make its début on the battlefield, even then in a form which promised much but delivered considerably less. The only alternative course of action would have been to stop the war, which was no alternative at all.

How, then, might the Generals have acted differently? Since 1918 sources as diverse as Lloyd George, the rock group Pink Floyd and the television comedy series *Blackadder* have promoted the canard that all British commanders were remote, even cowardly figures, preferring to direct each futile Big Push from the comfort of a well-appointed château deep inside the comfort zone, and far removed from the sharp end. But again, this is false history. In modern warfare it is not the role of senior commanders to lead from the front, or expose themselves to unacceptable levels of risk by making foolhardy tours of inspection of front line positions (although some, like Allenby, did). To do so would have been wholly irresponsible: ordinary troops can be trained in a matter of months, whereas the process of training and developing senior commanders is measured in years. Similarly their headquarters could hardly be sited within range of enemy guns. Besides which, a surprising number of British generals did become casualties during the conflict: no fewer than 78 were killed while on active service, and another 146 wounded. During the Battle of Loos (1915) alone, eight commanders above the rank of major-general became casualties, including one captured. And it should not be forgotten that most of the First World War generals had engaged the enemy more closely in previous campaigns when more junior in rank. The oft-told story that Lieutenant-General Sir Launcelot Kiggell burst into tears during 'his first visit' to the front at Passchendaele in November 1917 is almost certainly apocryphal.

Had Haig and his Staff subordinates attempted to direct their battles from positions nearer the front, they would have gained no advantage at all. A critical yet often ignored factor in the manner in which the First World War was fought is that it was the only conflict in history to have been fought without effective battlefield communications or voice control. It is a simple but irrefutable truism that without control the commander is unable to command. In 1914 the Royal Engineers signals service barely existed, and lost much of its equipment and cable stock during the retreat from Mons. Early wireless sets were the size of an ammunition limber, and scarcely field-portable beyond the location of a brigade or divisional headquarters. Field telephones were available, but suffered from at least two significant drawbacks. The first of these was that the cables were prone to being cut by shellfire, or by the iron-shod wheels of artillery or transport vehicles. Adverse weather and cable theft also worked to their detriment. By 1916 the Engineers had reached the conclusion that cables would only be secure from shelling when buried to a depth of six feet, although even that degree of hard labour offered no guarantees. Conditions at the front meant that breaks were often hard to locate, let alone repair, yet it was not uncommon for signallers to have to repair 40 or 50 cable breaks in a single day. The other problem was security, the official RE history published in 1921 acknowledging that more was given away to enemy eavesdropping in 1916 than during the previous year. Only in the last few months of the war did wireless finally come into its own, so that for almost the entire duration of the war communications between forward and rear areas relied upon such imperfect (and usually hazardous) means as runners, carrier pigeons, heliographs, semaphore flags and lamps, rockets, and messages dropped by aircraft. If smoke was used to screen an attack, the options were limited further still.

Once an attack was launched, communications with the advancing troops were reduced almost to zero. Pigeons, dogs and visual morse were seldom reliable, while markers – if visible – confirmed little more than the position reached by a particular unit. The greater burden fell on runners, whose chances of survival were much reduced when trying to cross open ground swept by shell, machine gun and sniper fire. In these conditions a message could take hours to reach its destination – up to six according to the *Official History*, by which time the position on the ground might have changed beyond recognition. The problem affected the Germans to a lesser degree, since on the Western Front theirs was essentially a defensive war, conducted from deep dugouts and trenches which benefited from relatively secure communication systems. During an assault, therefore, British commanders were more often than not unable to command and control, whether by way of committing reserves to exploit success, or to call off futile attacks, or – and this most crucially – to call down artillery support where needed. The problem was less one of incompetence than of impossibility. At the outset of the war the necessary technology simply did not exist, and by its close had still not reached a sufficiently advanced state of development.

German commanders faced equivalent problems and suffered comparable casualties, and not only in attack. In defending against the Somme offensive between July and October 1916 the German field army was grievously weakened, taking some half a million casualties, perhaps 150,000 of them killed. Two years later the *Kaiserschlacht* of March 1918 resulted in the final ruination of the German army, despite the fact that Ludendorff's forces had recently been greatly reinforced by stormtroops released from the Eastern Front, men well versed in offensive tactics, and attacking an understrength British army little used to defensive warfare. Popular history does not record that Ludendorff, von Falkenhayn and Hindenburg were fools and donkeys, despite the fact that German casualties between 1914 and 1918 were generally no less horrific as those suffered by the British under French and Haig. By the same token, infantry wastage rates in the Pacific and North West Europe were no kinder in 1944–45, when infantry battalions might lose half their strength in any given attack, and the life expectancy of the junior subaltern was also measured in weeks. Yet on the basis of this information it is seldom argued that Field Marshal Montgomery or his divisional commanders were tactically inept, or cared nothing for the lives of the men under their command. Indeed Haig and most of his commanders remained popular with their troops. Instead, it was the morale of the French army which collapsed in April 1917, resulting in widespread mutiny and refusal of duty.

As a commander Haig was much hampered by the need to comply with French demands, and meet time-scales which did not always match the needs of the BEF. Too often the British army was obliged to launch and sustain costly attacks for no better reason than the need to relieve pressure on their French and Russian allies. The inglorious attack at Loos between June and December 1915 was fought at the insistence of the French, with the somewhat remote object of assisting the Russians, who had lately been driven out of Warsaw. Haig predicted that the attack would end in disaster, and so it did. In mid-February 1916 the French agreed with Haig to make a combined push north of the River Somme on or about July 1st, on a front of twelve miles. Then, at the end of February, the Germans launched a powerful offensive at Verdun, which rapidly bled the French army white. As a result the French commitment to the Somme offensive shrank rapidly, while the BEF was required to take over more sections of the French line, and weakened correspondingly. Ten days after the Somme offensive opened with catastrophic losses, the fighting at Verdun eased considerably, which ranks as a success of sorts. But it is doubtful that any of the thousands of British and Allied casualties took much comfort from this. Again, in April 1917, the BEF suffered 150,000 casualties supporting the ill-fated French Nivelle offensive. This in turn led to a fatal delay in operations in Flanders, with the result that Third Ypres became bogged down in the mud of Passchendaele, where men came to believe that the thunder of the artillery was causing the clouds to unleash the torrential rain.

Popular myth portrays the machine gun as the greatest casualty-producer on the Western Front, but in fact the First World War was primarily an artillery war, and shells the bigger killer. The problem of effective coordination of infantry and artillery tactics remained acute from declaration through to Armistice. Prior to 1916 British artillery tactics were largely simplistic. By means of a long preliminary artillery bombardment – lasting seven days in the case of the push on the Somme – it was anticipated that all German targets engaged would be destroyed in advance of the main infantry assault, be they trenches, strong points, machine gun nests or wire belts. However, the expected result was not achieved for two principal reasons. The first was that even the heaviest bombardment was incapable of achieving total destruction, given how deeply the German defenders were dug in. The second was that the number of guns, as well as the type and quality of munitions, were wholly inadequate for the task in hand. During the early stages of the war the importance of heavy-calibre weapons was sorely underrated by British planners, the BEF of 1914 being able to field just six heavy batteries, as compared to 72 field batteries. By November 1918 the ratio had increased to 440 heavy or siege batteries, and 568 field batteries. Yet even by July 1916 the BEF could muster only one heavy gun per 57 yards of frontage. Although following the shell scandal of 1915 artillery munitions were no longer in chronically short supply, ordinary shrapnel shells were of limited effect against hard targets, and were of negligible value in cutting wire. High explosive was more effective, but decried in some quarters as unsporting, since it gave off yellow fumes which were rumoured to be poisonous. Far too many shells – up to a third – were duds which failed to explode, due in large measure to an exceptionally rapid expansion in manufacturing capacity in which quality had been sacrificed for quantity. Even after these several ills were remedied, high explosive shells tended to bury themselves in ground or mud before detonating, thus reducing their effectiveness and making the cratered moonscape of No Man's Land still more impenetrable. A remedy, in the form of the Model 106 impact fuse, would not be introduced until 1917.

Only after the holocaust of July 1st 1916 did the creeping barrage come to be widely adopted by the BEF. This technique involved a wall of exploding shells advancing ahead of the infantry, as well as covering its flanks, with the object of stunning and blinding the defenders, thus preventing them from taking effective action before the attacking infantry reached their lines. The intention was simply to neutralize the opposing enemy positions rather than carry out mass destruction; manuals suggested that infantry advance just 50 yards behind the barrage, although 20 or 30 yards was more usual. On ordinary ground it was reckoned that infantry could keep pace with a barrage which advanced at a rate of 100 yards every three to four minutes. In muddy conditions, troops were unlikely to keep pace even if the time between barrage lifts was extended to eight minutes. A combination of substandard or inappropriate munitions and inexpert gun-laying methods made the creeping barrage an imperfect science until 1917, while the pervasive curse of poor battlefield communications served as another significant limiting factor. Once the infantry moved out of visual range of the artillery observers in forward positions, it became nigh on impossible for the guns to regulate the speed of advance of the barrage in accordance with directions from the infantry, or to direct additional concentrations of fire where required. All that commanders and planners could do was try to second-guess the conditions and speed in advance.

Without voice control the creeping barrage was not without its flaws, and the very nature of the technique meant that troops were required to advance steadily in extended line. Yet as the quantity of guns increased in step with the quality of shells and gunnery, by trial and error these tactics began to reap dividends. The preliminary bombardment, comprising a correct munitions mix, could cut wire, destroy artillery and isolate enemy troops in forward trenches from food, munitions and reinforcements. The science of counter-battery fire improved beyond measure during 1917, by virtue of accurate mapping and weather forecasts, gun calibration centres and effective techniques for flash and sound location. False zero hours left the enemy uncertain of the timing of the attack, or its precise location, while the creeping barrage might consist of not one but five or six successive lines of fire, supported by a hurricane bombardment of trench mortars and barrage machine gun fire as the troops attacked. The 106 Fuse improved wire cutting and reduced 'back splash' from the barrage, allowing the infantry to follow even more closely. Ground–air cooperation with the Royal Flying Corps was refined, while by 1918 the use of smoke and gas shells became commonplace.

The result was that, after several hard lessons, the British army of late 1916 onwards was the most effective all-arms fighting force on the Western Front, and would remain so until victory in November 1918. Just as the disaster of the Dieppe raid in August 1942 taught the Allies any number of valuable lessons which paved the way for later successful seaborne landings in Sicily, Italy and Normandy, so the Somme may be seen as the crucible of the British army, and the subsequent refinement of artillery tactics positive proof that its commanders learned from past mistakes and eventually bettered their enemy.

Nevertheless, it remains the case that the problem of command and control was never substantially overcome, even as new technologies reached the battlefield. A telling example in this context was seen at Cambrai in November 1917 when the commander of the newly formed Tank Corps, Brigadier-General Hugh Elles, elected to lead his entire force of more than 400 vehicles into battle in person. In due course Elles rumbled across the start line in the leading tank of H Battalion, christened Hilda, proudly flying the Corps flag. While certainly admirable, the gesture rang hollow. Once the primitive ironclads took to the field, Elles quickly found that his command capacity inside Hilda was limited to a light kick delivered to the driver's left or right shoulder, depending on the change in direction required. After forging through the enemy wire Hilda became ditched, and Elles realised that if he wanted to influence the battle at all he had no option but to walk back to his headquarters at Beauchamp, where he could direct the battle with the aid of several field telephones. So this he did.

The tank itself gave rise to a wide variety of myths and legends, both during and after the war. The primitive Mark I 'land dreadnoughts' first trundled into action on 15th September 1916 during the middle stages of the Somme offensive, when two vehicles managed to penetrate as far as the target villages of Flers-Courcelette. An observer of the Royal Flying Corps reported back to GHQ that he had sighted 'A tank in the main street of Flers, with large numbers of troops following it.' This message was written up by the propaganda bureau, and famously appeared in the British press as 'A tank is walking up the High Street of Flers, with the British Army cheering behind it.' It was a fanciful image, but one which matched the high expectations of the then commander of the Heavy Branch of the Machine Gun Corps, General Ernest Swinton:

I imagined the consternation of the enemy – the feelings of the German machine gunner, by now accustomed, thumbs pressed on the double button of his gun, to mow down our oncoming infantry, while he in vain emptied belt after belt of ammunition against the strange monsters which loomed up out of the morning mist and came lurching and sliding on and on, over trenches and through wire.

Following the symbolic success of two tanks at Flers, unbounded public excitement about the exploits of the new war-winner persisted until the end of the conflict, and in the first few days gave rise to outlandish rumours. Among these short-lived myths were that each tank was at least as large as a house, manned by a crew of 400 men, was equipped with 12-inch guns, could travel at speeds of up to 30 miles per hour, and was built in Japan by Swedes. Other rumours were slightly less positive, it being said that the tanks were officered by Royal Flying Corps aircrew who had lost their nerve. Several no less outlandish rumours had circulated in the vicinity of Thetford earlier in the year while the Heavy Branch trained in conditions of great secrecy at Elveden, including one that a giant underground tunnel was being bored right through to Germany.

The myth of the tank as a war-winner endured rather longer. Writing to his wife in August 1918, Winston Churchill (by then the Minister of Munitions) appraised the tanks as 'invincible' machines that were sure to play a 'decisive' part in the Allied victory. Jean de Pierrefeu, an official at French General Headquarters throughout the war, wrote in 1923 that from the tank 'was to come victory as Pallas came from the head of Zeus'. If anything, the Germans proved even more effusive in their praise. Writing in his memoirs, the former infantry General A.D.H. von Zwehl affirmed that: 'I consider we were beaten not by the genius of Marshal Foch, but by "General Tank". In other words, a new weapon of war, in conjunction with the widespread reinforcement of the Americans.' Indeed for some time after the end of the war tanks were referred to in Germany as 'Germany's Death'.

In fact the reality of the tanks' first day of combat was very different. On September 15th only 49 tanks were combat ready, 13 of these breaking down before they could cross the start line. By July 1917 there were still only 136 operational vehicles available for the commencement of Third Ypres, colloquially known as Passchendaele. Even at Cambrai on 20th November 1917, when 378 tanks achieved spectacular success on the first day of the battle, legend holds that a single German artillery officer succeeded in disabling 16 tanks as they crawled over Flesquières Ridge, and no less than 56 per cent of the force as a whole was immobilized. The statistics for Amiens in August 1918 were if anything worse. Of the 342 Mark Vs which took to the field on the 8th, only 145 remained fit for action the following day. By the 10th only 85 were operational, and 38 on the 11th. On the 12th, enemy action, breakdowns and crew exhaustion meant that just six tanks were able to fight.

Conditions inside an operational tank were succinctly described as a pocket hell. One tank commander who took part in the first tank actions on the Somme in September 1916, Sir Basil Henriques, records:

> The nervous strain in this first battle of tanks for officers and crew alike was ghastly. Of my company, one officer went mad and shot his engine to make it go faster; another shot himself because he thought he had failed to do as well as he ought; two others had what I suppose could be called a nervous breakdown.

The simple truth was that the Mark I tank was a slow, cumbersome and unreliable machine, highly vulnerable to enemy attack, and when in transit or action a hellish operational environment for its eight-man crew. Basic mobility remained a fundamental problem. The maximum road speed of the Mark I was little more than 3.7 mph, which by 1918 had barely increased to 4.6 mph in the improved Mark V. Over broken ground, and in particular a cratered battlefield, a tank was unlikely to exceed 1.5 or 2 mph. Moving tanks from railheads and assembly areas to their start lines was a time-consuming process, with many breaking down en route due to mechanical defects. Tanks had to be refuelled with aviation spirit every 55 kilometres. Even steering and changing gear required considerable physical effort, and the active participation of most of the crew.

The tank was originally designed as an armoured 'machine gun destroyer', able to crush belts of wire and take out enemy strong points with ease, and minimal casualties. However, the armour of the Mark I was nowhere more than 12 mm thick, which from the outset made them vulnerable to an existing German rifle munition, the toughened 'K' round, developed to penetrate the steel loopholes used by British snipers. Even ordinary rounds could have considerable effect against the tank, particularly machine gun fire, for fragments of bullets tended to penetrate through gaps between the armour plates and other apertures, causing 'bullet splash'. Although seldom fatal, wounds inflicted in this way were usually extremely painful, and obliged crews to wear cumbersome face visors. Any hit from an artillery shell would knock out a tank, while in time the Germans found that a bag of grenades thrown under a tank stood a fair chance of blowing off the track. Large calibre 13 mm anti-tank rifles were issued to German troops in 1918, which could penetrate the armour of a Mark IV at 120 yards. All these factors combined meant that the tank was a weapon of very limited usefulness without infantry support, without which it was vulnerable, and was incapable of holding any ground taken. Tanks might break into enemy positions with relative ease, but breaking through them was quite another matter.

The peculiar geography of the Western Front after two years of trench warfare also greatly restricted the effectiveness of early tanks. The Mark I was constructed in the form of a rhomboid, with the tracks running around track frames larger than the hull situated between them. This design and track arrangement was intended to enable tanks to negotiate trenches and large shell holes, but at a weight of around 28 tons, tanks ditched easily in craters and trenches wider than ten feet, or bogged on soft ground, and were prone to 'belly' on tree stumps or similar obstacles. The terrain in the trench zone, coupled with the lack of springing, meant that tanks made for very poor gun platforms, and usually relied on crushing enemy positions rather than hitting them with their 6-pounders or machine guns. During the latter stages of the war tanks were also found to be of limited use in villages, where they were unable to engage targets above ground floor height, and where their weak top armour was exposed to grenade attacks.

These various factors conspired to achieve a proportionally higher casualty rate amongst tank crews than infantry. Besides which, the conditions inside a tank in action were nigh on intolerable. Tanks had no springs, and crewmen were liable to be injured simply by being thrown about inside the cramped fighting compartment. Indeed during one particularly vigorous demonstration for King George at a 'tankodrome' in France in 1917, all but one of the crew was knocked unconscious. Noise, heat and ventilation were also perennial problems. The basic tank of the Great War was little more than a steel box on tracks, with a large – and largely unshielded – 105 hp Daimler engine positioned in the middle of the cramped crew compartment. The deafening noise produced by the engine, tracks and guns meant that verbal communication between crew members was impossible, as General Elles discovered at Cambrai. Kicks and hand signals had to suffice inside the vehicle, while communication between tanks was reliant on semaphore and carrier pigeons until the first few wireless-equipped machines appeared in late 1917. The punishing interior temperatures, which could rise as high as 48 degrees centigrade, coupled with the noxious petrol fumes and carbon monoxide produced by the engine, meant that crews were generally rendered incapable after four hours in action. Crewmen were also liable to burn themselves on hot machinery, and even soldered joints could warp, releasing further noxious vapours. The Mark V, introduced in March 1918, increased speed and made steering manageable by the driver alone, but by lodging the radiator inside the hull without compensating ventilation intensified the problem. The ludicrous result was that conditions inside the troop-carrying version of the Mark V, in theory capable of moving 25 men towards the enemy line in conditions of relative safety, meant that the lucky few 'required a considerable time for recovery' before they could join the battle.

The oft-voiced criticism that Haig squandered the tactical and shock value of the tanks by committing them in 'penny packets' rather than a vast steel armada is also misplaced. Production of vehicles remained painfully slow, due in part to the position of the Admiralty, who were reluctant to release the necessary quantities of steel plate. Haig had no choice but to field tanks in small numbers in September 1916. The tank was then still an untried experimental weapon, which had to be tested in combat before thousands were ordered. The weather, and therefore the ground, was likely to deteriorate as the autumn wore on. Without tank support, it was inevitable that infantry casualties would have been heavier, while the memory of 57,000 on July 1st was still painfully fresh. The alternative, which was to hold the tanks in reserve, was no alternative at all, and would have seen Haig condemned still further. The negative view expressed by the likes of Swinton, Churchill and Liddell Hart that Haig's decision to use a small number of tanks was 'inexplicable' does not bear close scrutiny.

France actually produced more tanks than did Britain, although both the Schneider and Saint Chamond heavy types were failures, being under-powered, under-armoured and prone to catching fire. This is not to say that the British tank of 1916–18 was a white elephant, or that it did not play a major part in the final Allied victory. On the first day of the Cambrai attack on November 20th 1917, 378 combat tanks and 98 support vehicles (just three with wireless equipment) led an advance of 9,500 yards on a 13,000 yard front, at a cost of approximately 1,500 casualties. During the preceding campaign, Third Ypres, a similar advance by conventional means had taken three months and cost almost 400,000. Even when they performed poorly, the appearance of tanks on the battlefield reduced casualties and boosted the morale of Allied infantry, and often spread a good deal of alarm and despondency amongst the enemy. They also dispensed with the need for a prolonged initial artillery bombardment, which served to alert the enemy that an attack was due. Armour would become a decisive factor in countless battles during the next world war, and beyond. But assertions by German historians that 'General Tank' was a decisive factor in the defeat of the Kaiser's army have more to do with the need to find convenient scapegoats, than with historical fact. Indeed Ludendorff and his General Staff drew specific attention to the allegedly unstoppable power of the tanks only during the Hundred Days between August and November 1918.

Before leaving behind the vexed subject of the tanks, an exotic contemporary myth recorded by Swinton is worth repeating.

There is one persistent myth of which I think I can dispose – that of the secret [of the tanks] having been wormed out of some member of the Heavy Section and betrayed to the Germans by the so-called Javanese dancer, Mata Hari, who was executed as a spy by the French at Vincennes. I have read everything I have been able to obtain about her life and career, and have found no confirmation of the story. In fact, I do not think it was possible for her to have discovered the secret. Nor have I been able to find any corroboration of the equally romantic tale that it was communicated by another woman spy, one Fraulein Doktor, to a German technical officer, who would not listen to her warning and afterwards committed suicide in remorse at his mistake.

A story current at the time of Mata Hari's death [in 1916] was that two officers were heard talking: 'I say, old boy,' said one, 'you know everything. Who was it really gave away the secret of the tanks?' 'Why, the Japanese dancer – er – er – Hara Kiri, of course.'

The attitude of Douglas Haig to the tanks exposes the lie that he was a military Luddite, wholly uninterested in new weapons and technologies. On September 19th, four days after a single tank had reached Flers, Haig requested that a further 1,000 tanks be delivered to the Heavy Branch as quickly as possible. Following his experience in the Sudan in 1898 Haig was also an early champion of the machine gun, even taking two days out from his embarkation leave to visit the factory at Enfield, where he studied their manufacture and the mechanics of the Maxim. In August 1914 the allocation of a weapon frowned upon by some individual officers remained inadequate, at two guns per battalion, but this was hardly the fault of the generals. As early as 1909 the army had pressed for an allocation of six per battalion, but the proposal was rejected as too expensive by the then Chancellor of the Exchequer, David Lloyd George. As Director of Military Training at about the same time, an attempt by Haig to equip the army with other new technologies (grenades and trench mortars) was also refused. In September 1915, Haig pioneered the use of poison gas by British forces at Loos.

Legend holds that early in 1915 Haig dismissed the machine gun as 'a much overrated weapon' saying that 'two per battalion were more than sufficient', an accusation widely promulgated by Swinton and Liddell Hart from the 1930s onwards. However, the primary source, a memoir published in 1930 by the first commandant of the BEF machine gun school at St Omer, Brigadier-General Baker-Carr, is unreliable. Baker-Carr seems not to have directly identified Haig, and the original documents have never been available to modern historians such as John Terraine, who exposed the fallacy of many of the machine gun myths in *The Smoke and the Fire*. Far from being disinterested in automatic weapons, in September 1914 the War Office demanded that Vickers increase their production capacity five-fold, from 10 to 50 per week. In November the weekly figure was increased to 200, while in February 1915 another 2,000 guns were ordered from America, making a total order for almost 4,000. According to the mercurial Lloyd George, it took the generals 'many months of terrible loss' to realise the worth of the machine gun, but these statistics expose that statement as untrue.

Elsewhere Lloyd George appraised the machine gun as 'the most lethal weapon of the war', but this too is myth. Bullets from all sources accounted for only 38.98 per cent of British casualties, whereas shells and bombs accounted for 58.51 per cent. Each German 77mm shell shattered into 500 steel splinters, each a potentially lethal projectile. For the infantry it was therefore artillery which ranked as the principal terror of the war, rather than machine guns, mud, vermin or lice. Witness the diary of Sergeant-Major Frederic Keeling of the Duke of Cornwall's Light Infantry, in an entry written in December 1915:

In our brigade a man is damned lucky if he gets a dozen hours' sleep in three days in the trenches . . . It's trench mortars and whizz-bangs on and off all day and night in the intervals of bombardments. I don't pretend to have been through anything like as much as the men who have been out here 8 months and never missed the trenches, but I have been through enough to know what they have been through. And then people think it is mud and wet we mind; that is nothing, absolutely nothing, compared with the nerve-wracking hell of bombardment. Of course, people at home can imagine that more easily than the bombardments, so that is what they talk about.

Lloyd George distrusted – indeed detested – Haig with an unnatural vigour, and after becoming Prime Minister in December 1916 attempted several times to unseat him as Commander-in-Chief, but without success. An essential difference between the two men was that Haig and his generals wanted to win the war, and to win on the Western Front, whereas Lloyd George wanted merely to end it. In 1917 Lloyd George resorted to starving the BEF of replacement troops for its reserves and fighting divisions, despite the fact that by 1918 there were almost half a million fit and able soldiers in Britain. The result was that by January 1918 Haig's armies were 25 per cent understrength, which did much to contribute to the weakness of the 5th Army in particular, and the initial success of the German offensive in March. Indeed the Prime Minister was responsible for yet another enduring Great War myth, namely the idea that had the realities of trench warfare been known to the public at large, the war would have ended by sheer weight of public outrage. Lloyd George made explicit this opinion to C.P. Scott, the editor of the *Manchester Guardian*, over breakfast in December 1917:

> I listened last night, at a dinner given to Philip Gibbs on his return from the Front, to the most impressive and moving description from him of what the war in the West really means, that I have heard. Even an audience of hardened politicians and journalists was strongly affected. If people really knew, the war would be stopped tomorrow. But of course they don't know and can't know. The correspondents don't write and the censorship would not pass the truth . . . The thing is bloody horrible beyond human nature to bear and I feel I can't go on with the bloody business: I would rather resign.

It is undoubtedly true that most war correspondents conveyed to their readers little or nothing of the truth of the war on the Western

Front. Censorship was imposed on August 2nd 1914, and correspondents barred from the continent until the spring of 1915. Instead Lord Kitchener appointed Ernest Swinton, then a colonel in the Royal Engineers, to the staff of the Commander-in-Chief to prepare official reports on the progress of the conflict. These were heavily vetted before being released to the fourth estate under the byline 'Eye-witness', although many complained that 'Eye-wash' would have been a more appropriate pseudonym.

Meanwhile Kitchener ordered that any press correspondent ('drunken swabs') found in the field should be arrested, deprived of his passport and expelled. By early 1915 arrest warrants had been issued for a number of reporters mentioned by name: one such, the aforementioned Philip Gibbs, was kept under open arrest for ten days, then warned he would be shot if he returned to France. Haig blamed the shell scandal of 1915 on the presence of war correspondents in France and barred *The Times'* military correspondent Charles Repington from his 1st Army HQ. After it was realized that the stringent British reporting restrictions might have an adverse effect on public opinion in America, the first accredited correspondents arrived in France in June 1915. Nevertheless, by and large these men only reported what they were allowed to see (which was very little), and what they were permitted to write (which was even less). When in 1917 Repington published an article in the *Morning Post* criticizing Lloyd George and the Supreme War Council at Versailles, both writer and paper were prosecuted and fined £100. Indeed in the view of Arthur Ponsonby, the author of *Falsehood in Wartime*, there was 'no more discreditable period in the history of journalism' than the four years of the First World War. This view is borne out in a passage by the notoriously fatuous William Beach Thomas of the *Daily Mail* from July 1916, who in reporting British casualties on the first day of the Somme painted a ludicrous picture:

The very attitudes of the dead, fallen eagerly forwards, have a look of expectant hope. You would say that they died with the light of victory in their eyes.

In November, after the Somme offensive had ended, Thomas still found comfort in the perceived superiority of British corpses:

Even as he lies on the field he looks more quietly faithful, more simply steadfast than others, as if he had taken care while he died that there should be no parade in his bearing, no heroics in his posture.

A summary by Philip Gibbs in the *Daily Chronicle* on July 3rd was scarcely more truthful:

And so, after the first day of battle, we may say with thankfulness: All goes well. It is a good day for England and France. It is a day of promise in this war, in which the blood of brave men is poured out upon the sodden fields of Europe.

C.E. Montague, who served first in the trenches, and then as a censor, wrote the following of the myths promulgated by war correspondents in 1922:

The average war correspondent – there were golden exceptions – insensibly acquired a cheerfulness in the face of vicarious torment and danger. In his work it came out at times in a certain jauntiness of tone that roused the fighting troops to fury against the writer. Through his dispatches there ran a brisk implication that the regimental officers and men enjoyed nothing better than 'going over the top'; that battle was just a rough, jovial picnic; that a fight never went on long enough for the men; that their only fear was lest the war should end on this side of the Rhine. This, the men reflected in helpless anger, was what people at home were offered as faithful accounts of what their friends in the field were thinking and suffering.

Most of the men had, all their lives, been accepting 'what it says 'ere in the paper' as being presumptively true. They had taken the Press at its word without checking. Bets had been settled by reference to a paper. Now, in the biggest event of their lives, hundreds of thousands of men were able to check for themselves the truth of that workaday Bible. They fought in a battle or raid, and two days after they read, with jeers on their lips, the account of 'the show' in the papers. They felt they had found the Press out.

All of which was undoubtedly true. However, the idea that the public at home would have demanded an end to the war if faced with the truth is demonstrably false. Although much of the detail of campaigns such as Ypres, Neuve Chapelle, Loos, the Somme and Passchendaele was not widely known in Britain until the 1920s, casualty lists were published at the time, even in those urban centres in the industrial north of England where Pals Battalions were raised and subsequently decimated. The mounting numbers of widows, orphans and Blighty wounded were plain for all to see. The celebrated film by Geoffrey Mallins and J.B. McDowell, *The Battle of the Somme*, was released in cinemas in 1916 and included graphic scenes of trench warfare and dead British soldiers, and even footage of some as they fell. The population became hardened, even coarsened – but not disgusted or pacifist. Between April to September 1917 it was the morale of the French army which broke in spectacular fashion, not that of the British. The shortages caused by the German submarine blockade of Britain, particularly of food, seemed to both Vera Brittain and Siegfried Sassoon to be the main preoccupation of the British public, more so than the fighting in France.

It is a sad fact that the supreme achievement of the British and Commonwealth forces during the Hundred Days in 1918 are often ignored. Once the German offensives of March and April 1918 had stalled, Haig and his generals were able to reap the harvest sown during the previous two years. Between August and November Haig's armies won a series of battles which amounted to nine cumulative victories. After storming the Hindenberg Line they drove the enemy back from the Somme to the Sambre, in the process capturing 158,000 prisoners and 2,275 guns. Marshal Foch wrote that never had the British army achieved such spectacular results as it did during this continuous bodyblow offensive, which lasted 116 days, and was led by much the same generals who were damned as incompetent. An equivalent acknowledgement from Lloyd George was both late and grudging, Haig being congratulated only on October 10th on account of his achievements during 'the last few days'. The triumphant victories at the Scarpe, the Selle or the Sambre were never adequately acknowledged or conveyed to the public at large, and instead focus settled on the horrors of the Somme and Passchendaele. Simplistic denigration of the Generals and revelling in defeat may be more satisfying for some, and undoubtedly makes for better copy, but it does not tell the whole story of the First World War, or even the true one.

CHAPTER SEVEN

The Hidden Hand

Although a certain section of the population remained preoccupied with spy mania and the alien peril throughout the war, following notable peaks during August and September 1914, and again after the sinking of the *Lusitania* in May 1915, the delusion became more limited in its scope. One particular strand began to unravel from the paranoid whole, and to some extent may be seen as a forerunner of the conspiracy theories which we are familiar with today. This myth held that there existed a Hidden (or Unseen or Invisible) Hand, a covert pro-German influence at work in political, commercial and social circles, whose secret objective was to undermine the war effort, and paralyse the collective will of the nation.

During the winter of 1916 a series of meetings were held in London at which the government was denounced for its perceived inaction against this intangible menace. One meeting was called at the Queen's Hall by the Women's Imperial Defence League (WIDL) and was chaired by Frances Parker, sister of the late Lord Horatio Kitchener. Kitchener, architect of the so-called New Armies, had been killed in June 1916 en route to Russia when HMS *Hampshire* struck a mine off the Orkneys, an event which itself gave rise to a rich crop of legend. Some attributed his demise to the activities of highly placed Establishment spies, said to include the wife of Admiral Jellicoe, and riots broke out in Islington. Kitchener himself was said to have last been seen in an inappropriate embrace with a subordinate, while on Orkney itself the legend persists that the local lifeboat was ordered not to attend the stricken ship. Mrs Parker was among those not wholly convinced that her brother was dead: one theory ran that he was a prisoner in Germany, another more Arthurian variant was that he was deep in an enchanted asleep in a frozen cave, awaiting his country's next call. At the WIDL rally a resolution was passed which called for the immediate establishment of a Royal Commission to enquire into the activities of the Hidden Hand, coupled with a demand for the dismissal of all British diplomats with any links to Germany. In the Commons the Liberal MP for Cleveland, Herbert Samuel, urged fellow Members to do all in their power to try to dispel the 'foolish myth', but negatives are notoriously difficult to prove, and the meetings and rallies continued.

Just as the spy mania of 1914 had been fuelled by a sensationalist play, *The Man Who Stayed at Home*, now a patriotic film helped to boost public belief in the reality of an invisible hand. In *It is For England* (later reissued as *The Hidden Hand*) offered up a young army chaplain reincarnated on the battlefield as St George returns to England to harangue the nation on the Teutonic peril. As well as addressing Parliament (a scene in which extras were joined by real MPs), St George also states his case to City businessmen and industrial rebels. Backed by the Navy League, the film also featured many of the mythical spy devices which had made *The Man Who Stayed at Home* such a populist hit.

A measure of the credulous atmosphere in which these popular protests took place was given by the diarist and *Times* journalist Michael McDonagh, writing on December 1st 1916:

> The news editor, Gordon Robbins, rushed into the reporting room this morning shouting that he had got a delicious letter in reference to the 'Hidden Hand' meeting last night . . . It said: 'I have to tell you of a discovery we made at our meeting tonight. A German spy was found taking notes of the speeches. When questioned he pretended to be a reporter from *The Times*, and was disguised as a Nonconformist minister. I enclose the card he gave us.'
>
> The card was Jack Turner's, an old member of the reporting staff . . . His story, as he told it in his serious way, was very funny. He

was sitting alone at the Press table, taking notes of the chairman's opening remarks, when a woman in a high state of excitement, leant over his shoulder and looking at his note-book, asked peremptorily what he was writing. 'Shorthand' was his simply reply. 'That is not shorthand; I know Pitman; it's German,' the woman exclaimed, snatching the note book. Turner writes in an old system of shorthand, called Taylor's, which at a casual glance might well be mistaken for German characters.

The woman interrupted the proceedings with a loud shout of 'Mr Chairman, there's a German spy here,' and throwing the note-book to the chairman, added, 'Look at that!' The chairman and others on the platform examined the note-book, and for a time appeared to be suspicious as to its purpose, but in the end gave it back to Turner in exchange for his card.

Whereas the main focus of spy mania remained aliens and foreigners, enemy or otherwise, the myth of the Hidden Hand tended to throw suspicion on Britons, many of them senior Establishment figures. Somewhere in between these two extremes fell the fantastical 'poison plot' of 1917, the denouement of which was the trial at the Old Bailey of four highly unlikely individuals charged with conspiring to murder David Lloyd George and his Minister Without Portfolio, Arthur Henderson, by means of darts tipped with curare.

Alice Wheeldon, aged 51, was a dealer in second-hand clothes who lived with her daughter Harriet, a scripture teacher, in the Midlands railway town of Derby. Both were ardent socialists, and prior to the outbreak of war had been active Suffragettes in the Women's Social and Political Union. Both mother and daughter opposed conscription, and Alice Wheeldon's home became a safe haven for conscientious objectors and other fugitives on the run from military service. Indeed her son William was already in custody as a hard-core conscientious objector, having refused to perform national service of any kind. The pair also helped to smuggle evaders abroad to Ireland and America, and had links with various radical groups including the Socialist Labour Party, and far-left union officials deported from Clydeside by governmental decree. The Wheeldons were rank-and-file radicals who displayed a high degree of disaffection, and occupied a lower-middle class milieu in which feminism, socialism and pacifism found common cause.

In December 1916 a man calling himself Alec Gordon sought shelter with the Wheeldons. He claimed to be a fugitive, and having won their confidence introduced the two women to one Comrade Bert, who in turn claimed to be an army deserter and a member of the Industrial Workers of the World. In fact both men were agents employed by a special intelligence section within the Ministry of Munitions, whose activities were later absorbed within the Special Branch and MI5. 'Alec Gordon' was the false identity of Mr F. Vivian, and 'Comrade Bert' a more senior agent named Herbert Booth, a former barrister's clerk. Both operatives subsequently laid information that Alice Wheeldon was plotting to assassinate Lloyd George on the grounds that he was the politician behind conscription and the Military Service Acts. To achieve this end Wheeldon had obtained some poisons from her son-in-law, Alfred Mason, a laboratory attendant at Hartley University College in Southampton, thus drawing him and her other daughter Winnie Mason into the plot. Alfred Mason, aged 24, was said to share the views of his relatives on the general conduct of the war, and circumstantial evidence suggests that Alice Wheeldon had made arrangements to secure his passage to America when his call-up came.

The poisons provided by Mason arrived in Derby by post in January 1917, together with directions for use. The four phials contained both strychnine and curare, the latter an unusual poison which is harmless if taken internally, but deadly when introduced into a wound. The toxin was said to operate on the nerves and muscles, causing paralysis, and eventually death, through failure of the respiratory system. The poison came from South American tree bark, where it was used on arrows by Indians. Chief among its advantages was that it left no trace which could be identified by analysis or post mortem examination of the victim. At trial it would be alleged that Alfred Mason was 'a chemist of very considerable skill' who had made a special study of poisons generally and curare in particular, the qualities of which were known to very few.

Together with Alice Wheeldon and her two daughters, Mason was charged under the Offences Against the Person Act 1861 with conspiring to murder Lloyd George and Henderson, and with soliciting Herbert Booth to carry out the killing. The Attorney-General himself appeared for the prosecution, and all four defendants entered pleas of Not Guilty. Of the Ministry agents, only Booth gave evidence at trial. By his account, which was uncorroborated, the Wheeldons were hardened political terrorists who had burned down a church in Breadsall, and tried to kill Reginald McKenna, the Chancellor of the Exchequer between 1915 and 1916, by sending him a skull containing a poisoned needle. Alice Wheeldon was also said to have observed the need to kill Lloyd George:

Lloyd George has been the cause of millions of innocent lives being sacrificed. He shall be killed to stop it. We Suffragettes had a plot before when we spent £300 in trying to poison him. Our idea was to get a position in an hotel where he was staying and drive a nail through his boot that had been dipped in poison; but he went to France.

The evidence offered by Alice Wheeldon was at some variance. By her version, the poison was needed to kill guard dogs at the 'concentration camps' where conscientious objectors were being held, although for the Crown a Major Kimber stated that nowhere were dogs used for this purpose. Although Alice Wheeldon denied the charges, her words and conduct in court did her defence few favours. On one occasion, the judge, Mr Justice Low, disdainfully noted 'a considerable amount of levity' in the dock, and instructed defending counsel to caution his clients. In evidence, Alice Wheeldon stated that in sheltering 'COs' she knew she was breaking the law, but did not mind for she had a perfect right to help circumvent what she considered an iniquitous act:

Q: Have you a strong feeling against those specially responsible for introducing this iniquitous Act of Parliament?

A: Yes.

Q: And in particular against Mr Lloyd George?

A: Yes.

Q: And you regard Mr Henderson as a traitor to the working classes?

A: I have said so.

Q: And your feeling towards Mr Lloyd George is one of the strongest possible antagonism – would it be true, for instance, to say that you hate Mr Lloyd George?

A: I do (This answer was given with energy).

Q: You would like to do him a mischief?

A: He's not worth it.

Q: But if he was, you would?

A: Yes.

Q: Do you mean that?

A: I feel very strongly against him.

Q: Bitterly?

A: Yes.

Q: And you think it would be a good thing if his career came to an end?

The witness was understood to assent with the qualification 'public career'. She expressed her belief that the Prime Minister had done immense harm, was a source of mischief particularly to the working classes, and had been the occasion of the sacrifice of thousands of lives. She considered that he ought to be punished, severely punished. She did not remember saying that the ******* should be killed to stop it. She admitted that she had spoken of the Prime Minister in very obscene terms, and admitted that one particularly foul expression put to her by the Attorney-General was a favourite mode of her expressing her disapproval. She had said he ought to be killed. Pressed on the point, however, she said she did not think it now, adding 'We often say in our bitterness things we do not mean.' She meant it at the time.

Q: And did you say that another who ought to be done in was George of Buckingham Palace?

A: Very likely.

Q: And you meant it?

A: I did at that time in my bitterness.

Q: Have you changed your opinion since?

A: I refuse to answer the question.

In further cross-examination, Alice Wheeldon said she did not think that from first to last anything was said to Booth about dogs. She denied that she had ever said that Walton Heath would be the best place to catch Lloyd George with an air gun. At that time she did not know that Mr Lloyd George's house at Walton Heath had been burned down by Suffragettes.

The trial lasted five days, which included the re-opening of the case before a reconstituted jury owing to the illness of one of the original members. In his summing-up, defending counsel, a Mr Riza, submitted that the prosecution was 'scandalous, vile and vindictive' and an affront to public justice. Riza made much of the fact that 'Alec Gordon' had not been produced to the court, and ventured that the employment of 'mysterious secret government agents' was un-British. Bizarrely, Riza then suggested that in keeping with the odd and somewhat farcical nature of the case, the proper mode of trial should be trial by ordeal:

LOW   I am afraid that has been abolished.

RIZA   That is why I submit it to the jury.

LOW   You cannot submit it to the jury.

RIZA   I think it is my duty.

LOW   That the ladies should walk over hot ploughshares or something of that kind? Is that it?

RIZA   I do suggest that, Mr Lord, in order that they may prove their innocence.

LOW   It is no use putting that. If you have anything serious to suggest I should like to hear it.

Mr Riza concluded by saying that the prisoners were English to the backbone. It was ridiculous to suggest that Mr Lloyd George could have been killed by poisoned arrows or darts. He claimed a verdict of acquittal.

The jury took just 30 minutes to return verdicts of Guilty against Alice Wheeldon, Alfred Mason and Winnie Mason, who received terms of imprisonment of ten, seven and five years respectively. Harriet Wheeldon was acquitted. In passing sentence, the judge observed that he could not think of a worse case, and that Alice Wheeldon had been convicted on evidence which could only have brought the jury to one conclusion. Turning to Alfred Mason, Mr Justice Low declared that but for the recommendation to mercy from the jury, he too would have received ten years' penal servitude. Of Winnie Mason he said that he took her upbringing into account, and that her position was due largely to the 'bad and wicked' influence of her mother. The coarse language habitually and admittedly used by all three women greatly irritated the judge, who, in noting that Harriet and Winnie were teachers, informed the jury he wondered whether elementary education was such a blessing after all.

After sentence had been passed, Sylvia Pankhurst was allowed to enter the witness box to deny that the Suffragette movement had ever spent £300 on a plot to murder the Prime Minister. Alice Wheeldon and the Masons each served two years in gaol before being released after a Home Office review, conducted at the express request of Lloyd George. In recent years commentators have observed that the defendants were convicted on doubtful evidence, although it should be borne in mind that traffic in lethal poisons was admitted, only the purpose being disputed. Alice Wheeldon's fanatical zeal for gesture politics had certainly run too far to avoid prosecution. Weakened by a meagre prison diet, hard labour and a succession of hunger strikes, she succumbed to influenza shortly after her release from custody in 1919. However, her legend lives on in the realm of fiction, informing both a play by Sheila Rowbotham (*The Friends of Alice Wheeldon*), and in *The Eye in the Door* (1993), the second volume of the acclaimed *Regeneration* trilogy by Pat Barker.

If aspects of the Wheeldon trial bordered on the ludicrous, it paled when compared to another case heard at the Central Criminal Court a year later, in June 1918. The nature of the action was unusual enough: the private prosecution of an MP by a dancer for criminal libel, following the staging of a banned play by Oscar Wilde. But it was the allegations which formed the background to the case that truly set it apart: that the Hidden Hand was seeking to undermine the British fighting spirit by propagating vices which 'all decent men thought had perished in Sodom and Lesbia', and to render the British army ineffective by the deliberate spread of venereal disease.

The background to this inglorious yet celebrated legal episode requires no little elaboration. In 1918 Noel Pemberton-Billing, the Independent MP for East Hertfordshire, had held his seat for two years and gained a reputation as a prominent demagogue. Billing, or 'PB' as he preferred to be known, was a man of many talents. A former repertory actor and singer, Billing was also an incorrigible inventor whose unlikely creations ranged from a pencil which calculated 'as you write' to a machine for making and packing self-lighting cigarettes, as well as the 'Digit Typewriter' and the 'Proxy Phone'. Billing also tried his hand at magazine publishing, farming, property development and a career at the Bar, all without conspicuous success.

In 1912 PB took a crash course in flying, obtained a pilot's licence, and founded the Supermarine Aircraft Company at Southampton, later to produce the Spitfire. Success was slow in coming for the company, however, and after war broke out PB decided to pursue a parliamentary career. Rejected by the Conservatives as a maverick, Billing stood as an Independent in the Mile End by-election, his stated aim being a 'strong air policy'. After losing to a Coalition candidate, and vexed by the lack of official interest in the designs generated by Supermarine, Billing enlisted in the Royal Naval Air Service (RNAS). His service career is somewhat mysterious: he was said to have taken a prominent role in the planning of the first bombing raid on Germany in November 1914, which targeted the large Zeppelin base at Friedrichshafen on Lake Constance, and to have risen to the rank of Squadron Commander.

Later, official sources would claim that Billing had spent only 12 months in the RNAS, had never flown on a raid or in the face of the enemy, and never rose beyond Flight Lieutenant. Whatever the truth, in March 1916 Billing fought and won the East Hertfordshire by-election, again as an Independent candidate, and with rude enthusiasm set about fulfilling what he described in his autobiography (published a year later) as 'the self-appointed task'.

By virtue of persistent questions in the Commons on air policy, Billing became known as the 'Member for Air', an ironic sobriquet which acknowledged his verbal profligacy, be it on the subject of spies, aliens or any other mild or serious cause for complaint. Billing vigorously promoted his self-image of a man of action, drove a lemon-yellow Rolls Royce, dressed in unusual clothes, and expressed a preference for 'fast aircraft, fast speed-boats, fast cars and fast women' – and kept quiet the fact that his wife, Lilian Schweitzer, was half-German. To further his cause for a greater degree of 'purity' in public life, and to root out the 'mysterious influence' of the Hidden Hand, Billing founded a small-circulation subscription-only journal called *The Imperialist*, which he initially ran at a loss from his Hertford base, and which carried inflammatory articles intended to provoke libel writs, and thus self-serving publicity. For this reason no advertising revenue was forthcoming for the magazine, although a measure of financial backing was provided by Lord Beaverbrook. In June 1917 Billing also founded the Vigilante Society, and proved himself to be a combative character in a more literal sense. A month afterwards, a slighting reference to army officers made in the Commons triggered a confrontation with Colonel Archer-Slee, which ended that evening in the two men exchanging punches on the grass in New Palace Yard. Escapades of this kind failed to impress his political superiors, who regarded Billing as a loose cannon. Indeed, in the opinion of David Lloyd George: 'This man is dangerous. He doesn't want anything.'

Although Billing and his self-appointed task appeared patriotic to a fault, his vision was clouded by something far darker. Many of the political radicals from whom he drew inspiration, and who were employed or published by his magazine, were engaged in developing what is identified by author Philip Hoare as a virulent strain of British fascism. Henry Beamish, who ran the Vigilante Finance Committee, was a hardened anti-semite who preached that the German jews, or Ashkenazim, had infiltrated British society at all levels. Dr J.H. Clarke, another founding Vigilante, was chief consulting physician at the Bloomsbury Homeopathic Hospital; his self-proclaimed mission was to protect England from the Church of Rome. No less unpleasant was Arnold White, an elderly editor of the *English Review* whose ideas embraced the forced Jewish colonisation of Argentina, and whose books included *The Modern Jew*, *Efficiency and Empire*, *Is the Kaiser Insane?* and *The Hidden Hand*. The latter, published in September 1917, was particularly popular, its lurid black cover and shocking red lettering offering a stern warning to all right-thinking Britons. On the subject of pervasive treachery, White wrote:

> You deny the existence of the Hidden Hand. I have seen the criminal finger-marks of the Hidden Hand in Downing Street, in the Foreign Office, in the Home Office, in the Admiralty, in the Board of Trade, in the Local Government Board, in the headquarters of the County Constabulary, and in the Cabinet itself. The difference between an educated man and a half-educated man is the difference between perception and detection of truth and willingness to believe what one wants to believe. Disinterested study of evidence is the touchstone of statesmanship. You aver that the Hidden Hand is a myth. Lawyers and party politicians are no less liable to error than disinterested students of public affairs.

White goes on to quote from a letter written by him to the Home Secretary, Herbert Samuel, in February 1916:

> For the last year I have had incessant complaints from Brighton and Hove of the extent to which Germans and pro-Germans are encouraged. The enclosed postcard, insulting the British Army, was bought to me in the presence of two witnesses on Saturday the 19th inst., at a shop of a German who was interned last year.

On his internment he placed his brother in charge – a pure German. This man has recently been in Scotland, and has been granted an armlet to excuse him from service.

From this underwhelming (and unspecified) evidence, White concluded:

If there is no Hidden Hand, what was the force that enabled the Brighton Hun to affront the people of Sussex by insult to the British Army and then boast of his immunity?

A later article by White on the subject of 'Efficiency and Vice' so impressed Billing that it was reprinted in *The Imperialist* in December 1917. The gist of this curiously garbled call-to-arms was that the combination of German efficiency and decadence amounted to a moral invasion of England, by which the 'stamina' of Britain's youth was being undermined. White warned of unspecified 'vices of the Cities of the Plain', in respect of which 'Palestine taught nothing to Potsdam': Germany was said to be in a state of total moral degeneracy owing to the all-pervasive power of homosexuals, referred to as 'urnings'. According to White, at London District Command, a dedicated team of 'very able Intelligence officers' was engaged in fighting the infection of Londoners, and troops in particular, with the doctrines of the German urning:

Espionage is punished by death at the Tower of London, but there is a form of invasion which is as deadly as espionage: the systematic seduction of young British soldiers by the German urnings and their agents . . . Failure to intern all Germans is due to the invisible hand that protects urnings of enemy race . . . When the blond beast is an urning, he commands the urnings in other lands. They are moles. They burrow. They plot. They are hardest at work when they are most silent . . . Men are willing to die for their homes, but if the conception of home life is replaced by the Kultur of urnings, the spirit of the Anglo-Saxon world wilts and perishes.

The myth of Teutonic homosexuality was scarcely new, and even permeates the pages of *Greenmantle*, John Buchan's second Richard Hannay thriller published in 1916. While it is true to say that the years 1914–18 saw a significant increase in cases of male indecency brought before the courts, this had no more sinister cause than the simple fact that large numbers of young men were herded together under wartime conditions. White, however, discerned the presence of the Hidden Hand. Although his purple portrait of gay subversion was pure fantasy, it proved too much for Beaverbrook, who chose to sever all connections with *The Imperialist* in mid-January 1918. By way of response, Billing elected to push the myth of a homosexual Hidden Hand further still.

PB had by this time employed a new assistant editor, Captain Harold Spencer. Spencer had been invalided out of British military intelligence, where he claimed variously to have undertaken secret service work in the Middle East, acted as aide-de-camp to the King of Albania, Prince William of Wied, and to have served as a captain in the Royal Irish Fusiliers. Latterly, said Spencer, he had been trained as a pilot, but little if any of this history was true: Spencer had been discharged from the service in September 1917 suffering from paranoid 'delusional insanity', and was now labouring under a deep (and probably pathological) sense of injustice. He complained to Billing of having been badly treated by his superior officers and higher authorities, who had refused to take his outlandish conspiratorial theories seriously.

Like White, Spencer was convinced that the manhood of Britain was being 'exterminated' by the German urning menace, and he appears to have been generally preoccupied with decadence, homosexuality and gynaecology. With the aid of a large body of information supplied by Spencer, Billing ran a lengthy and outrageous article in *The Imperialist* for January 26th 1918:

THE FIRST 47,000
There exists in the Cabinet Noir of a certain German Prince a book compiled by the Secret Service from reports of German agents who have infested this country for the past 20 years,

agents so vile and spreading such debauchery and such lasciviousness as only German minds can conceive and only German bodies execute.

It is a most Catholic list. The names of Privy Councillors, wives of Cabinet Ministers, even Cabinet Ministers themselves, diplomats, poets, bankers, editors, newspapers proprietors, and members of His Majesty's Household. The officer who discovered this book while on special service [i.e. Spencer] briefly outlined for me its stupefying contents. In the beginning of the book is a précis of general instructions regarding the propagation of evils which all decent men thought had perished in Sodom and Lesbia. The blasphemous compilers even speak of the Groves and High Places mentioned in the Bible. The most insidious arguments are outlined for the use of the German agent in his revolting work.

As an example of the thoroughness with which the German agents work, lists of public houses and bars were given which had been successfully demoralised. These could then be depended upon to spread vice with the help of only one fixed agent. To secure those whose social standing would suffer from frequenting public places, comfortable flats were taken and furnished in erotic manner. Paphian photographs were distributed, while equivocal pamphlets were printed as the anonymous work of well-known writers.

Agents were specially enlisted in the navy, particularly in the engine rooms. These had their special instructions. Incestuous bars were established in Portsmouth and Chatham. In these meeting paces the stamina of British sailors was undermined. More dangerous still, German agents, under the guise of indecent liaison, could obtain information as to the disposition of the Fleet. Even to loiter in the streets was not immune. Meretricious agents of the Kaiser were stationed at such places as Marble Arch and Hyde Park Corner. In this black book of sin details were given of the unnatural defloration of children who were drawn to the parks by the summer evening concerts . . . Wives of men in supreme position were entangled. In lesbian ecstasy the most sacred secrets of State were betrayed. The sexual peculiarities of members of the peerage were used as a leverage to open fruitful fields for

espionage. In the glossary of this book is a list of expressions . . .
used . . . by the soul-sick victims of this nauseating disease so
skilfully spread by Potsdam.

If anyone was 'soul-sick' it was surely the delusional fantasist Harold
Spencer, who had clearly given much energy to the construction of
an imaginary world in which gay brothels, lesbian trysts, wanton
sailors and indecency with children were commonplace. Like much
of the copy which appeared in *The Imperialist* (which in February
was re-born as *The Vigilante*), his extraordinary article was intended
to trigger a civil libel writ that would further Billing's self-appointed
task. The charge that the lives of three million Britons in France had
been betrayed by the perverse carnal tastes of 47,000 of their
countryman could hardly be less serious, or more calculated to
attract headlines. But despite the fact that Billing sent copies to
selected ministers and government departments, no writs or other
censure materialized, and the article was said to have caused hilarity
in the trenches.

Instead, the Vigilantes seized an unexpected opportunity to drag
their cause through courtroom doors. In February 1918 it was
announced by a minor theatrical producer, Jack Grein, that two
private performances of Oscar Wilde's *Salome* would be staged in
London in April. The play had long been banned by the Lord
Chancellor as blasphemous, and Grein's production was given an
added frisson by the fact that the actress cast as Salome was Maud
Allan, a daring dancer from America long famous for her exotic
performance piece, *The Vision of Salome*. Allan had performed her
dance with great success in London in 1908, its popular success due
in large part to her voluptuous figure and revealing costume. The
name of Oscar Wilde, of course, remained synonymous with
decadence and the love that dare not speak its name – even by
urnings. Allan was rumoured to be a lesbian, or bisexual, and was
known to have dined with the Asquiths, who had supported the
posthumous rehabilitation of Wilde. Against this background, it was
scarcely surprising that the proposed staging of *Salome* did not pass
unnoticed by Billing and his coterie.

Spencer moved quickly. After contacting a local doctor to enquire after an appropriate anatomical term, he graced the front page of *The Vigilante* for February 16th with the following paragraph:

THE CULT OF THE CLITORIS
To be a member of Maud Allan's private performances in Oscar Wilde's *Salome* one has to apply to a Miss Valetta, of 9 Duke Street, Adelphi, W.C. If Scotland Yard were to seize the list of these members I have no doubt they would secure the names of several of the first 47,000.

Neither Grein nor Allan saw the piece until three weeks later, but on doing so instructed solicitors immediately. On March 8th a judge in chambers granted leave for the pair to commence criminal proceedings for both obscene and criminal libel. This move rattled Billing, who had reckoned only on a civil libel action and a modest claim in damages, rather than a Crown prosecution and the prospect of a maximum of two years' penal servitude. Nevertheless, although a third charge of defamatory libel was added at a later date, Billing continued to fire lurid broadsides from the pages of *The Vigilante*. On March 23rd, for example, its small band of readers was warned of the methods by which the Hidden Hand were spreading venereal disease:

The German, through his efficient and clever agent, the Ashkenazim, has complete control of the White Slave Traffic. Germany has found that diseased women cause more casualties than bullets. Controlled by their Jew-agents, Germany maintains in Britain a self-supporting – even profit-making – army of prostitutes which put more men out of action than does their army of soldiers.

But by now the British armies in France and Belgium were facing a far graver challenge than the clap. On March 21st the long stalemate in the trenches was brought to an abrupt end by a massive German assault on the Western Front. The attack fell mainly on the British Fifth Army, which was sent reeling in the face of 59 German divisions, many of them released from the Eastern Front following the negotiated peace with Russia. During the first week the Germans advanced 40 miles, and by the beginning of June had reached the Marne to threaten Paris. The Allied situation was more critical than at any time since September 1914. In panic, the War Cabinet talked of pulling back to the Channel ports and evacuating all British troops back to England.

In this climate spy mania and anti-alien sentiment reached fever pitch. Like Billing and his Die-Hard ilk, the Northcliffe press stepped up its campaign to 'Intern Them All' and make 'a clean sweep' of individuals of enemy origin from public office. The campaign, and others like it, also called for the closure of German businesses and banks, and a boycott of German goods. Local councils up and down the country began to pass resolutions endorsing like measures, while July saw mass anti-alien rallies in Trafalgar Square, Hyde Park and the Albert Hall, as well as the Free Trade Hall in Manchester. In August, the groundswell of support for total internment was such that a 'monster petition' some two miles in length and containing more than a million signatures was delivered to Downing Street by lorry, accompanied by a veritable three-ring circus.

The Billing libel case opened at Bow Street Magistrate's Court in April, and after PB entered a plea of justification was committed to the Old Bailey for trial in May. During the intervening period an already complicated plot had thickened further. After it emerged that Lloyd George was engaged in secret peace negotiations with the German foreign minister, Billing was approached by *The Times*' influential military correspondent, Colonel Charles Repington. Talk of peace outraged the Generals, who found allies in the British far right. Repington suggested that Billing get his trial postponed, and use the mythical 'Black Book' to smear senior politicians and inflame anti-alien feeling in the Commons. By this logic, the current peace talks would be ruined and Lloyd George's authority undermined. He would be brought down, leaving the Generals to take control of the War Cabinet and run the war as they wished.

The government, in turn, attempted to spike Billing by means of a female *agent-provocateur*, Eileen Villiers-Stuart, whose purpose was to lure PB to a male brothel in Duke Street. Here, it was hoped, Billing would be compromised, or at least observed, and his parliamentary career immolated in a blaze of scandal. It was a textbook example of fighting fire with fire, although the plan was destined to backfire after Villiers-Stuart fell in love with Billing and became his mistress.

The trial opened at the Old Bailey on May 29th before Mr Justice Darling, who seems to have been specifically assigned to the trial. Billing chose to conduct his own defence, a move which did much to ensure that every conceivable strand of paranoid Vigilante nonsense was drawn out in evidence, and that the proceedings swiftly degenerated into farce. The six-day trial attracted wide press coverage, chiefly because of the novelty of a high-profile MP being sued by an exotic dancer, and the supposed existence of the Black Book containing 47,000 names of famous people, all said to be at risk of blackmail due to moral weakness and perverse sexual predilection. The legendary book, of course, was never produced. A climax of sorts was reached on the second day when Eileen Villiers-Stuart, who claimed to have been shown the Black Book by two army officers over afternoon tea in Ripley in the summer of 1915, revealed certain of the names in open court:

> Billing suddenly banged the table with his fist, dramatically pointed at the Judge, and he and Villiers-Stuart began shouting at each other at the tops of their voices.

> PB: Is Justice Darling's name in the book?
> VS: (shouting) It is.
> JD: Just a moment.
> VS: (still shouting) It can be produced!

> Considerable commotion in court. Cries of 'Order' by the ushers.

> JD: It can be produced?

Villiers-Stuart, waving her hand wildly at the Judge, and Billing, still with hand outstretched, continued shouting at the tops of their voices.

VS: It can be produced; if it can be produced in Germany, it can and shall be produced here. Mr Justice Darling, we have got to win this war, and while you sit there we will never win it. My men are fighting, other people's men are fighting-

PB: Is Mrs Asquith's name in the book?

VS: It is.

PB: Is Mr Asquith's name in the book?

VS: It is.

PB: Is Lord Haldane's name in the book?

VS: It is.

At which point Darling belatedly intervened, and ordered Villiers-Stuart to leave the witness box. She did not, and from this point on the judge lost control of the court. Villiers-Stewart went on to claim that Jack Grein was a German agent, and that her two officer friends from the Ripley tearoom had been murdered in Palestine on account of their detailed knowledge of the contents of the Black Book. Billing next called Harold Spencer, the delusional former intelligence officer from whose disordered mind had sprung the 'First 47,000' and the 'Cult of the Clitoris'. Spencer claimed to have seen the Black Book while perusing the private papers of Prince William of Wied in Albania in 1914. Examined by Billing he told the court:

PB: Did you see the list of public houses and baths, and recognise the names of any of them in London?

HS: Yes, that was gone into with Admiralty Intelligence. Admiralty Intelligence did their best to close the whole matter as far as they could . . . They conducted a very thorough campaign and I believe stamped out part of the German system here in London.

PB: Were these German agents using these public houses, and baths and massage establishments?

HS: I believe our Intelligence has evidence they were.

PB: You said in the article that the names of 'Privy Councillors, youths of the chorus, wives of Cabinet Ministers, dancing girls, even Cabinet Ministers themselves, while diplomats, poets, bankers, editors, newspaper proprietors, and members of His majesty's household follow each other with no order of precedence. . .' Do you stand by that on oath?

HS: On oath.

Spencer went on to state that Margot Asquith and Lord Haldane appeared on the list, but declined to name others. Darling took no effective action to stop these irrelevant smears, on the dubious premise that his own name had already been blackened. Spencer went on to inform the judge that Wilde's play *Salome* was 'pure sadism', which he defined as the lust for dead bodies.

PB: Are you aware that it is only perverts who practise these vices?

HS: I do not know if the German agents are really perverted.

PB: Do you mean they practise them even against their own will in the interests of their own country?

HS: Against their own instincts, I should think.

JD: What do you mean; do you think the German agents practise these things?

HS: If a German agent is instructed to practise sodomy by his chief, probably he does.

PB: Do they succumb?

HS: I know they do.

PB: How do you know?

HS: Through the Intelligence; through the Admiralty.

PB: They practise this to bring into bondage English people?

HS: That is their object, apparently.

PB: And these perverts are people who take an interest in all sorts of sexual inversion. Do you know of your own knowledge that only pantomime performances of unnatural passion appeal to the German people?

HS: The Intelligence people think so.

THE HIDDEN HAND 171

When cross-examined by prosecuting counsel, Travers Humphreys, Spencer spouted yet more psycho-sexual claptrap:

TH: You stated in your cross-examination that Miss Maud Allan was administering the cult . . . Will you tell the court exactly what you meant by that?

HS: Any performance of a play which has been described by competent critics as an essay in lust, madness and sadism, and is given and attracts people to it at from five guineas to ten guineas a seat, must bring people who have more money than brains; must bring people who are seeking unusual excitement, erotic excitement; and to gather these people together in a room, under the auspices of a naturalised alien [i.e. Grein], would open these people to possible German blackmail, and that their names, or anything that transpires, might find their way into German hands, and these people would be blackmailed by the Germans; and it was to prevent this that the article was written.

Elsewhere, Spencer was asked:

TH: What necessity was there for heading this statement 'the Cult of the Clitoris'?

HS: In order to show that a cult exists in this country who would gather together to witness a lewd performance for amusement during wartime on the Sabbath . . . The Cult of the Clitoris meant a cult that would gather together to see a representation of a diseased mad little girl.

TH: Just think what you are saying.

HS: I have.

TH: The clitoris is part of the female organ?

HS: A superficial part.

TH: In which the sexual sensations are produced?

HS: It is what remains of the male organ in the female.

TH: Do you mean to tell my Lord and the jury that when you wrote those words . . . you meant anything more than this, the cult of those sensations by improper means.

HS: I meant superficial sensations which did nothing to help the race.

TH: By improper methods, methods other than the ordinary connection between man and woman?

HS: Than the usual connection between man and woman. An exaggerated clitoris might even drive a woman to a bull elephant.

Thus ran the defence. The cast of bizarre 'expert' witnesses paraded by Billing also included Dr John Clarke, who offered that *Salome* should be stored in a museum of sexual pathology, and even then might corrupt medical students. A fashionable Jesuit priest, Father Bernard Vaughan, testified that the play constituted a 'constructive treason', and even shook Billing's hand as he left the box.

In his lengthy final address to the jury, Billing again warned of the all-pervading influence of the Hidden Hand:

How much more necessary is it that the light of day should be let in? How much more necessary is it that the influence – the mysterious influence – which seems to have dogged our footsteps through the whole conduct of this campaign; the influence which, after three and a half years of war, keeps German banks still open in this country, leaves Germans uninterned in this court at the present minute, the influence which for two and a half years paralysed the Air Service of this country, and prevented us raiding Germany. Is it not time that this influence was removed?

I am a libeller. I have libelled public men for the last two and a half years . . . Gentlemen of the jury, I assure you that there must be some reason for all the 'regrettable incidents' of this war . . . What is the position in France today? It is worse than it was in August 1914. The best of the blood in this country is already spilled; and do you think that I am going to keep quiet in my position as a public man while nine men die in a minute to make a sodomite's holiday?

Billing tarred Maud Allan and *Salome* as part of the 'mysterious influence' of the Hidden Hand in the following terms:

Such a play . . . is one that is calculated to deprave, one that is calculated to do more harm, not only to young men and young women, but to all who see it, by undermining them, even more than the German army itself.

Billing sat down to great applause from his numerous supporters in the public gallery, having delivered an undeniably effective emotional harangue to the jury. Little if any of it was relevant to his plea of justification, but no matter: Darling's inept handling of the evidence ensured that PB's ulterior political purpose had been served. From then on until the close of the trial, Maud Allan was observed to be in tears.

On June 4th, amidst scenes of uproar in the courtroom, Billing was acquitted. Hardly ever had a verdict been received in the Central Criminal Court with such unequivocal public approval. The crowd in the gallery sprang to their feet and cheered, as women waved their handkerchiefs and men their hats. On leaving the court in company with Eileen Villiers-Stuart and his wife, Billing received a second thunderous ovation from the crowd outside, where his path was strewn with flowers. Even had Billing been convicted he would have still succeeded in his political object. In the event, although some editors berated Billing for his methods, the ends were generally seen to justify the means, and to represent a famous victory for patriotism, morality and the common man.

But not everyone was as delighted. The diary of Cynthia Asquith for early June well reflects the horrified reaction of the political establishment, and the Asquith family in particular:

One can't imagine a more undignified paragraph in English history: at this juncture, that three-quarters of *The Times* should be taken up with such a farrago of nonsense! . . . It is monstrous that these maniacs should be vindicated in the eyes of the public . . . Papa came in and announced that the monster maniac Billing had won his case. Damn him! It is such an awful triumph for the 'unreasonable', such a tonic to the microbe of suspicion which is spreading through the country, and such a stab in the back to people unprotected from such attacks owing to their best and not their worst points. The fantastic foulness of the insinuations that Neil Primrose and Evelyn de Rothschild were murdered from the rear makes one sick. How miserably conducted a case, both by that contemptible Darling and Hume Williams! Darling insisted on having the case out of rotation.

Billing's famous victory proved short-lived. Although membership of the Vigilante Society swelled dramatically in the wake of the trial, the peace talks were scuppered by the sinking of the hospital ship *Llandovery Castle* at the end of June, and so Billing became surplus to the Generals' requirements. The Enemy Aliens Act was passed in July, while by September it was clear that Germany was exhausted, and that her army was beaten. Billing had been forcibly removed from the Commons after a row on the subject of internment in July, and in 1921 resigned his seat on grounds of ill health. He died in 1948, having devoted much of the rest of his remarkable life to writing, sailing, inventing, and managing a cinema.

The fate of the other leading characters was equally mixed. In September 1918 Eileen Villiers-Stuart was convicted of bigamy, and sentenced to nine months' hard labour. In a sworn statement she admitted that the evidence she had given in the Maud Allan trial was entirely fictitious, and that she had rehearsed it with Billing and Spencer. Spencer returned to the courts in 1921, where he was convicted of libel following the publication of an anti-semitic article in the journal *Plain English*. He was sentenced to six months in gaol, and stripped of his army rank by the War Office. A few months after his release Spencer was convicted of unspecified 'disgusting behaviour' and fined 40 shillings. Maud Allan went abroad, and did not return to Britain until 1928. By 1939 she was living in comparative poverty in a section of the West Wing, a large mansion on Regent's Park. Curiously she was allowed to remain after the house was requisitioned by the army, and after the house was damaged during the Blitz returned to the USA on the Lisbon clipper flight, a miraculous achievement under wartime conditions. In 1956 she died in obscurity in a Los Angeles nursing home. Suspicions linger that the government sponsored Allan and Grein in their libel action, with the object of ensuring that Billing and his cohorts fell from grace in the immediate aftermath. The whole truth, however, may never be known.

Postscript

Having surveyed the panoply of myths and legends of the First World War, it is striking just how many were repeated or mirrored during the Second World War, two decades later, in many instances down to the last detail.

This is particularly true of several Home Front myths which arose as a result of spy mania and general xenophobia during the opening months of each conflict. In 1940, as in 1914, spies were thought to lurk around every corner, and to be signalling furiously to enemy aircraft and submarines. The Hidden Hand became the Fifth Column, dachshunds appeared in newspaper cartoons with swastikas drawn on their backs, and pigeon fanciers once more fell under suspicion. Shops, restaurants, cafes and ice cream parlours owned by Germans and Italians were boycotted, stoned and looted, while commercial printers sold posters which declared for the benefit of purchasers that 'This Firm is Entirely British'. Despite the passage of time, and widespread disenchantment following the exposure of many calculated falsehoods in the years after 1918, credulity and spitefulness again held sway over certain sections of the population. Just as the spies of 1915 seemed often to betray their true calling by wearing extravagant hats and capes, so one army subaltern was denounced by a vicar's daughter in London for failing to flush the lavatory at his rectory billet – to her mind, a sure sign of Hunnish Kultur.

Other second war myths of 1940 differed in form, but not in substance. Kaiser Wilhelm's vaunted insanity became Adolf Hitler's missing testicle, while the Russian troops with snow on their boots were replaced by the multitudinous German corpses washed ashore on the south and east coast in the wake of the Battle of Britain. Indeed the parallels between these two early wish-fulfilling myths is particularly illuminating. For several weeks during September and October 1940, all Britain was gripped by a rumour that an attempted German invasion had been thwarted in the Channel, and that tens of thousands of corpses had arrived at various points between Cornwall and the Wash. As with the Russians a quarter-century earlier, everyone knew someone who had seen the bodies on the beaches, whose numbers grew exponentially with each week that passed, and whose existence was only half-heartedly denied by the War Office. The 1940 rumour gained a second wind when it was added that the sea had been set on fire with burning oil, with the result that the 40,000 corpses now became charred.

As with the elusive Russian horde, the lack of hard evidence or convincing eyewitness accounts of the presence of tens of thousands of foreign bodies on English soil did nothing to damp public enthusiasm for this satisfying yet absurd tale. Both myths appear to have arisen spontaneously, and then to have been adopted by official sources with the object of boosting morale, one in the wake of the Retreat from Mons, the other following disaster at Dunkirk and the fall of France. Although the Bowmen and Angels of Mons have no obvious second war counterpart, the almost supernatural notion that the British were capable of setting the sea on fire perhaps has something in common with the earlier legend inspired by Arthur Machen.

Hate propaganda was less vigorously promoted between 1939 and 1945, not least because the single Crucified Canadian was replaced by whole nations in Eastern Europe broken on the wheel of Nazism, while the fictive horrors of the corpse factory paled beside the bestial reality of the death camps. The issue of whether lingering cynicism over First World War atrocity myths resulted in the Allies ignoring the truth of the Final Solution for too long remains one of the great unanswered questions of modern history, although it is difficult to see what difference it would have made after September 1939. Indeed it is worthy of note that during the German blitzkrieg through Belgium and France in 1940 tales of butchered babies, outraged women and drunken looting were conspicuous only by their absence. Tellingly, the two survivors of the massacre of unarmed prisoners from the Royal Norfolk Regiment at Le Paradis in May 1940 by SS troops were disbelieved when they first reported the incident, on the basis that theirs was a 'cock-and-bull' story, and that Germans 'would not do that sort of thing'.

In time of war the lie becomes a patriotic virtue, and to some extent can enjoy only a limited half-life once peace is restored. But many of the more innocent First World War myths – those not deliberately manufactured, and never officially denied – have endured far longer, and remain in rude health even as they approach their centenary, having lost little of their remarkable regenerative power.

Source Notes

INTRODUCTION

CHAPTER 1

7   'The London Gazette . . .' McDonagh (1935), p. 15

7   'Indeed the grocers . . .' Haste (1977), p. 115

7   'German prostitutes . . .' Turner (1980), p. 30

7   'Famously, dachshund . . .' Greene (1971), pp. 48–9

7   'As early as . . .' *Eastern Daily Press*, 10 August 1914

8   'All I could . . .' McDonagh (1935), p. 15

8   'On October 18th . . .' Haste (1977), p. 114

8   'The riots triggered . . .' Haste (1977), p. 126

8   '. . . in Keighley' Macdonald (1987), pp. 210–12

9   'A large section . . .' McDonagh (1935), p. 32

10   '. . . Staffordshire Yeomanry' *Daily News*, 29 August 1914

10   'Articles and correspondence . . .' *The Times*, 5 September 1914

11   'For as the Commons . . .' Hansard, 3 October 1914

11   'What about the Press . . .' McDonagh (1935), p. 33

12   'Miss Gold . . .' Clark (1985), p. 38

12   'Given a British . . .' Thomson (1922), p. 40

13   'In October 1914 . . .' Turner (1980), p. 58

13   'Is it too much . . .' *Daily Mail*, 3 October 1914

13   'One celebrated . . .' Turner (1980), p. 58

14   '. . . and by September' *The Times*, 30 September 1914

14   'On Tuesday afternoon . . .' *The Times*, 3 September 1914

14   'At Maldon . . .' Horn (1984), p. 37

15   'It was not safe . . .' Thomson (1922), p. 44

15   'Similarly, in Norfolk . . .' Horn (1984), p. 37

15   '. . . DH Lawrence' Haste (1977), p. 121

15   'Even the First . . .' Stafford (1997), pp. 56–7

16   '. . . private correspondence' Stafford (1997), pp. 54–5

16   'The scare was given . . .' Thomson (1922), p. 38

16   'Monday 27 . . .' Clark (1985), p. 85

17   'Friday 3 . . .' Clark (1985), p. 81

17   'A popular . . .' Turner (1980), p. 60

17   'At this period . . .' Thomson (1922), p. 39

17   'Thomson also . . .' Dudley (1960), p. 147

18   '. . . in Cumberland' Rimell (1984), p. 30

18   'Hearing a swishing . . .' *Hackney & Kingsland Gazette*, 1960s (letter)

18   '. . . at Silvertown' *After the Battle*, Issue 18

19   'As time wore . . .' Thomson (1922), p. 41

19   '. . . the blackberries' Dakers (1987), p. 45

19   'Mayfair . . .' Turner (1980), p. 57

19   'Another spy was . . .' Turner (1980), p. 57

19   '. . . agony column' Thomson (1980), p. 42

20   'Later in the war . . .' Thomson (1922), p. 42

20   '. . . Maggi Soup' Thomson (1922), p. 40; Turner (1980), p. 58

21   '. . . some 400 people' Aston (1930), p. 82

21   'During many months . . .' Callwell (1920), pp. 33–4

21   'The legend of the . . .' Thomson (1922), p. 39

21   'The Daily Mail . . .' Haste (1977), p. 113

22   'Thomson describes . . .' Thomson (1922), p. 45–6

22   'An oft-repeated . . .' Thomson (1922), p. 41

22   'Another common version . . .' Thomson (1922), p. 41

22   'One apocryphal . . .' McDonagh (1935), p. 34

22   'In Braintree . . .' Clark (1985), p. 124

22   '. . . Hunnish perversions' *The Times*, 2 September 1914

23   'In consequence of . . .' *The Times*, 29 August 1914

23   'This afternoon . . .' Clark (1985), pp. 111–12

23   'One unfortunate . . .' Playne (1931), p. 267

24   'A clique . . .' Dakers (1987), p. 45

24   '. . . Rothenstein' Dakers (1987), p. 45

24   'The writer D.H. . . .' Haste (1977), p. 121; Dakers (1987), p. 66

25   'In the Suffolk . . .' Horn (1984), p. 37

25   'Near Woolwich . . .' Thomson (1922), pp. 44–5

26   '. . . the Crown Prince' Turner (1980), p. 62; Haste (1977), p. 122

26   'Blood is said . . .' *John Bull*, 24 October 1914

27   '. . . Baden Powell' Turner (1980), p. 62

27   '. . . Graham-White' Turner (1980), p. 62

27   '. . . Sir Hector Macdonald' Royle (1982)

27   '. . . Lord Haldane' Turner (1980), p. 59; Haste (1977), p. 123

28   'Every kind of . . .' Haldane (1929), pp. 282–3

28   '. . . Margot Asquith' Hoare (1997), pp. 86–8

28   '. . . no fewer than 50' Turner (1980), p. 60; Collins (1998)

29   '. . . John Buchan' Buitenhuis (1987), pp. 109–10

30   'Arthur Conan Doyle . . .' Buitenhuis (1987), pp. 110–11

Chapter 2

31   'At Carlisle . . .' Turner (1980), p. 53

31   '. . . at Durham' Turner (1980), p. 53

31   '. . . at Crewe' Turner (1980), p. 53

31   '. . . at Folkstone' *Daily News*, 1 September 1914

31   '. . . the Kiel Canal' Turner (1980), p. 53

31   'It was even . . .' Turner (1980), p. 53

32   'Successive variations . . .' Clark (1985), pp. 9–16

32   'In Perthshire . . .' Baden-Powell (1973), p. 100
33   '. . . in Cardiff' Turner (1980), p. 52
33   'A correspondent told . . .' *Daily News*, 1 September 1914
33   'Sir George . . .' Wilson (1986), p. 161
33   'Only that day . . .' Brittain (1933), p. 97
33   'Some people . . .' Hammerton (1938), pp. 86–6
34   'In letters from . . .' Wemyss (1935), p. 173
35   'There is being . . .' McDonagh (1935), pp. 21–2
35   'Many people here . . .' Bertie (1924), pp. 30–3
35   'Indeed when . . .' *Daily News*, 9 September 1914
36   'There is no . . .' *Daily News*, 15 September 1914
37   'London is depressed . . .' McDonagh (1935), pp. 23–4
38   'There was nothing . . .' Thompson (1922), p. 38
38   'M is full . . .' Charteris (1931), p. 38
39   'Tennant: I am . . .' Hansard, 18 November 1914
39   'The Russians in . . .' Charteris (1931), pp. 75–6
40   'This started . . .' Lovat (1978), pp. 78–9
40   'One held . . .' McDonagh (1935), p. 24
40   'Interestingly, MI5 . . .' *The Times*, 19 November 1997
40   'Another explanation . . .' Ponsonby (1928), p. 63
40   'From Paris . . .' Bertie (1924), p. 69
40   'It is also said . . .' Cockfield (1998), p. 2
40   'If so, as . . .' Hart (1930), p. 101
41   '. . . Sukhomlinoff' Ponsonby (1928), p. 63
41   'In his lengthy . . .' Churchill (1923), p. 224
41   'The outstanding . . .' Aston (1930), p. 73
42   'On September 5th . . .' Hart (1930), p. 100
42   'At this time . . .' Aston (1930), p. 75
43   'He wrote all . . .' Thomson (1922), p. 123
43   'Will you kindly . . .' Sellers (1997), p. 21
43   'In Edinburgh . . .' Sellers (1997), pp. 21–2
44   'Despite all his . . .' Deacon (1969), p. 181

CHAPTER 3

47   'Then there is . . .' Charteris (1931), pp. 25–6
47   'If any angels . . .' Richards (1964), p. 19
48   'I had the most . . .' Collins (1915)
48   'We came into action . . .' *Daily Mail*, 14 September 1915
49   'We had almost . . .' *Evening News*, 11 August 1915

50   'Arthur Machen . . .' see Charlton (1963)

50   'I looked out . . .' Hammerton (1938), p. 86

51   'during a particularly . . .' *Evening News*, 29 September 1914

52   'Whether Mr Machen's . . .' *Light*, 24 April 1915

52   'Later in April . . .' *The Universe*, 30 April 1915

53   'At least six . . .' Buitenhuis (1987), p. 104

53   'As late as 1966 . . .' Taylor (1966), p. 29

53   '. . . while in 1980' Terraine (1980), p. 18

54   'Owing to the . . .' Gibbs (1923), p. 217

55   'One vociferous believer . . .' Turner (1980), p. 56

55   'Another clergyman . . .' Wilson (1986), p. 161

55   'General N . . .' *Light*, 8 May 1915

55   '. . . one Mons veteran' Haythornthwaite (1992), p. 373

55   'A Nonconformist . . .' Turner (1980), p. 56

56   '. . . Forest of Mormal' Whitehouse (1964)

56   'Poor Dix . . .' *Light*, 7 August 1915

57   'Of first hand . . .' McClure (n.d.)

57   '. . . Margaret Woods' Playne (1931), p. 257

58   'The capture of . . .' MacDonald (1987), p. 212

58   'I have been at . . .' Charteris (1931), p. 75

60   'The Angels of Mons . . .' *Daily News*, 17 February 1930

60   'Curiously, the . . .' Howe (1982), p. 46

61   'Doidge, a veteran . . .' *Sunday Times*, 11 March 2001

61   'Now and again . . .' Bladud, 9 June 1915

64   'They looked out . . .' *Fate* magazine, May 1968

65   'Perhaps six or eight . . .' *Spaceview* magazine (NZ), April 1965

66   'The truth of . . .' McCrery (1992), pp. 68–81

67   '. . . Neuve-Chapelle' Blunden (1928), p. 54

68   'In the course . . .' McCrery (1992), pp. 69–70

68   'We are to . . .' McCrery (1992), p. 113

CHAPTER 4

70   'Later historical . . .' Terraine (1980), p. 23

71   'Boy scouts . . .' *The Times*, 2 September 1914

72   '. . . a court in Aachen' Read (1941), p. 93

73   'We bought . . .' Bloem (1930), pp. 20–1

73   'Bloem admitted . . .' Tuchman (1962), p. 310

74   '. . . Brand Whitlock' Terraine (1980), p. 28

74   '. . . boiling oil' Macdonald (1987), p. 208

74   '. . . exploding cigars' Read (1941), p. 62

74   '. . . 30 officers' Terraine (1980), p. 26
74   '. . . soldiers' eyeballs' Haste (1977), p. 85
74   'At Vise . . .' Read (1941), p. 91
75   'Some of the . . .' Read (1941), p. 91
75   '. . . Dinant' Tuchman (1962), pp. 308–9
75   '. . . Louvain' Tuchman (1962), pp. 311–16
76   '. . . an American diplomat' Terraine (1980), p. 29
76   '. . . deathless epithet' Read (1941), p. 58
76   'An hour before . . .' quoted by Terraine (1980), p. 29
77   '. . . 5000 civilians' Read (1941), p. 103
77   '. . . as at Nimy' MacDonald (1987), p. 136
77   'The distribution . . .' MacDonald (1987), p. 209
79   'In France . . .' Knightley (1982), p. 67
80   'On August 25th . . .' Gilbert (1994), p. 42
80   'She had literally . . .' Gilbert (1994), p. 42
80   '. . . destroy Christianity' Haste (1977), p. 83
80   'You will hear . . .' Haste (1977), p. 85
81   'Up the main . . .' Corbett-Smith (1916)
82   '. . . Grace Hume' Haste (1977), p. 84; Read (1941), pp. 37–8
82   '. . . although the times' The Times, 30 September 1914
82   'In addition to . . .' Collins (1998), p. 185
82   'In the Hands . . .' Collins (1998), p. 186
83   '. . . War, Red War' Collins (1998), p. 187
83   'Armageddon . . .' Collins (1998), p. 186
83   'A Belgian writer . . .' Read (1941), p. 35
83   'The Germans in . . .' Clark (1985), p. 22
83   '. . . five American' Read (1941), p. 29
84   'I was in . . .' Read (1941), p. 30
84   'Lord Northcliffe . . .' Haste (1977), p. 87
84   'The few photographs . . .' Ponsonby (1928), pp. 135–9
84   '. . . Grunewald' Haste (1977), p. 88
84   'In France . . .' Read (1941), p. 14
84   '. . . Lord Bryce' Peterson (1939), p. 58; Messinger (1992), pp. 71–84
85   'Even before . . .' Messinger (1992), p. 77
87   'As I looked . . .' Peterson (1939), p. 55
87   'We saw . . .' Peterson (1939), p. 56
87   'Immediately after . . .' Peterson (1939), p. 55
88   'Even in papers . . .' Peterson (1939), p. 58
89   'Your report . . .' Wilson (1986), p. 183
89   'A set of . . .' see Bland (1915)
89   '. . . H.C. Peterson' Peterson (1939), p. 58

90   'The public has . . .' Morgan (1916), pp. 61–3
90   'As regards . . .' Morgan (1916), pp. 58–9
90   '. . . White Book' Haste (1977), p. 95
91   '. . . Telconia' Haste (1977), p. 39
91   '. . . Matthias Erzberger' Erzberger (1920)
91   '. . . U27' Gray (1994), p. 238; Halpern (1994)
92   '. . . treated as felons' Simpson (1972), p. 40
92   '. . . Zeppelin L19' *Guardian*, 4 April 2001
92   '. . . Edith Cavell' Buitenhuis (1987), p. 29; Haste (1977), pp. 89–90
92   '. . . Marguerite Schmidt' Haste (1977), p. 90; Knightley (1982), p. 66
93   'The cold-blooded . . .' Haste (1977), p. 90
93   '. . . Austrian trench club' Haythornthwaite (1992), p. 374
93   'One Belgian . . .' Mead (2000), p. 19
93   '. . . league of scientific' Haythornthwaite (1992), p. 374
93   'as at Sabac' Gilbert (1994), p. 41
93   '. . . no shortage' *see* Reiss (1916)
94   '. . . the Holocaust' Fussell (1975), p. 316
94   'Finding now . . .' Ponsonby (1928), p. 26
94   'In 2001 . . .' *Guardian*, 11 May 2001

CHAPTER 5

96   '. . . extinction-level' McDonagh (1935), p. 16; *Daily News*, 15 August 1914
96   '. . . Michael McDonagh' McDonagh (1935), p. 16
96   'Also current . . .' Playne (1931), pp. 255–6
96   'The public . . .' *The Times*, 15 August 1914
97   'August 31st . . .' Clark (1985), p. 11
97   '. . . paid rent' Fussell (1975), p. 121
97   'November 9th . . .' Clark (1985), p. 30
98   'A stranger . . .' Blunden (1928), p. 115
98   'I remember . . .' Coppard (1980), p. 69
99   '. . . station master' Grant (1918), p. 141
99   '. . . Belgian women' Grant (1918), p. 47
99   'It was during . . .' Grant (1918), pp. 269–74
99   'During four long . . .' Sitwell (1949), pp. 8–9
100   'At Fresnes . . .' Beaman (1920), pp. 187–8
103   'Any information . . .' Hansard, 12 May 1915
103   'James Caldwell . . .' Clark (1985), pp. 61–2
104   'The Los Angeles . . .' Trumbo (1939), p. 23
104   'On the 14th . . .' Gilbert (1994), p. 162
104   'Another private . . .' Gilbert (1994), p. 162

104 '. . . Maple Copse' Fussell (1975), p. 117
105 'The Canadians fought . . .' *Plymouth Evening Herald*, 15 May 1915
105 'Showing that . . .' Hansard, 19 May 1915
106 'He . . . told me . . .' Scott (1922)
107 'The story . . . began . . .' Charteris (1932), p. 75
107 '. . . Vera Brittain' Brittain (1933), p. 374
107 'Another poet . . .' Tippett (1984), p. 82
107 'In 1915 Ian . . .' Hay (1915), p. 199
107 'He told me . . .' Clark (1985), p. 91
107 '. . . Prussian Cur' Tippett (1984), p. 82
107 'A later American . . .' Ponsonby (1928), pp. 184–5
108 '. . . immediately protested' Tippett (1984), p. 83
108 'By April . . .' Tippett (1984), p. 84. The full statements are on record at the National Archives of Canada.
110 '. . . Harold Peat' Peat (1918), pp. 149–50
110 'Ernest Chambers . . .' Tippett (1984), p. 82
110 '. . . Major G.C. Carvell' Tippett (1984), p. 86
110 'In June 1920 . . .' Tippett (1984), p. 87
110 '. . . until 1988' *see* Ward (2001)
110 'by Overton' *Sunday Express*, 15 April 2001
111 '. . . problems remain' Ward (2001)
112 'Quite a pleasant . . .' Asquith (1968), p. 44
113 'We have known . . .' *The Times*, 17 April 1917
115 'Other correspondents . . .' *The Times*, 26 April 1917
115 'The Lancet . . .' *The Times*, 20 April 1917
115 'Elsewhere both . . .' Ponsonby (1928), p. 103
116 'The letter told . . .' Sanders and Taylor (1982), p. 146
116 'The Germans protested . . .' *The Times*, 23 April 1917
116 'Dillon: Has . . .' Hansard, 30 April 1917
117 '. . . while the Daily Mail' Turner (1980), pp. 186–7
117 '. . . Rudyard Kipling' Turner (1980), p. 186
117 'The usually . . .' Turner (1980), p. 187
118 'No reasonable . . .' *The Times*, 17 May 1917
118 'Its director . . .' Sanders and Taylor (1982), p. 147
118 'At the Foreign . . .' Sanders and Taylor (1982), p. 147
118 'While it should . . .' PRO file, FO 395/147
119 'The relevant Foreign . . .' PRO file, FO 395/147
119 'In his authoritative . . .' Fussell (1975), p. 116
119 'Worldwide . . .' These Eventful Years, p. 381
120 'In the First . . .' Montagu (1970), pp. 31–2
120 'One day there . . .' *New York Times*, 20 October 1925

122   'The New York . . .' *New York Times*, 20 October 1925

122   'On arrival in . . .' *The Times*, 4 November 1925

123   '. . . Phillip Knightley' Knightley (82), p. 90

123   'This paper makes . . .' Ponsonby (1928), pp. 112–13

124   'Kenworthy: Does the . . .' Hansard, 24 November 1925

124   'Sir Austen . . .' Hansard, 2 December 1925

125   'Of all this . . .' Montague (1922), pp. 92–4

CHAPTER 6

127   'Alan Clark . . .' Terraine (1980), p. 170

128   '. . . war poets' Sheffield (2001), p. 15

128   'It is not too . . .' Lloyd George (1936), pp. 2038–9; p. 2040

130   'By no means . . .' Neillands (1999), pp. 244–5

130   'Indeed on the right . . .' Neillands (1999), p. 249, 261

130   'The total weight . . .' Edmonds (n.d.), pp. 313–14

132   '. . . no fewer than 78' Neillands (1999), pp. 19–20

132   'The oft-told story . . .' Neillands (1999), p. 223

132   'It is a simple . . .' Griffith (1998), pp. 7–8

134   'By the same token . . .' Brooks (1998), p. 19

135   '. . . just six heavy' Griffith (1998), p. 24

136   '. . . yellow fumes' Griffith (1998), p. 25

136   'Far too many . . .' Neillands (1999), p. 238

136   'Even after . . .' Griffith (1998), p. 12

136   'On ordinary ground . . .' Griffith (1998), p. 11

137   'The science of . . .' Griffith (1998), p. 13

138   'In due course Elles . . .' Terraine (1980), pp. 179–80

138   'This message was . . .' Neillands (1997), p. 285

138   'I imagined the . . .' Swinton (1932), p. 284

139   'Among these short-lived . . .' Swinton (1932), p. 291

139   'Several no less . . .' Swinton (1932), p. 242

139   'Writing to his wife . . .' Terraine (1980), p. 148

139   'Jean de Pierrefeu . . .' Swinton (1932), p. 11

139   '. . . ADH von Zwehl . . .' Swinton (1932), p. 11

140   'The nervous strain . . .' *The Times*, 16 September 1976

142   'The Mark V . . .' Terraine (1980), p. 149

144   'There is one . . .' Swinton (1932), p. 248

144   '. . . factory at Enfield' Terraine (1980), p. 139

145   'Baker-Carr . . .' Terraine (1980), pp. 134–5

145   'Far from being . . .' Terraine (1980), p. 137

145   'According to the . . .' Lloyd George (1936), p. 357
145   '. . . 38.98 per cent' Terraine (1980), p. 132
145   '. . . 77mm' Sheffield (2001), p. 92
145   'In our brigade . . .' Laffin (1988), p. 192
146   'The result was that . . .' Neillands (1999), pp. 447–52
146   'I listened last night . . .' Knightley (1982), p. 93
147   'Censorship was imposed . . .' Knightley (1982), pp. 69–79
147   '. . . Eye-wash' Knightley (1982), p. 70
147   'By early 1915 . . .' Knightley (1982), p. 78
147   '. . . 1st Army HQ' Farrar (1998), p. 70
147   'When in 1917 . . .' Neillands (1999), p. 456
147   '. . . Arthur Ponsonby' Ponsonby (1928), p. 134
147   'The very . . .' Laffin (1988), p. 74
148   'And so . . .' Farrar (1998), p. 106
148   'The average war . . .' Montague (1922), pp. 97–8
149   'The shortages . . .' Farrar (1998), p. xiii
149   'Marshal Foch . . .' Brooks (1998)
150   'An equivalent . . .' Brooks (1998)

CHAPTER 7

151   'One such . . .' Turner (1980), p. 241
151   '. . . in Islington' Haste (1977), p. 129
152   'In the Commons . . .' Turner (1980), p. 241
152   'It Is For England . . .' Turner (1980), p. 241
152   'The news editor . . .' McDonagh (1935), pp. 151–2
153   Alice Wheeldon trial: Rowbotham (1986); McDonagh (1935), pp. 180–1; The Times, 7–12 March 1915; Turner (1980), pp. 244–5
159   Pemberton Billing trial: Hoare (1997); Kettle (1977); Turner (1980)
161   'You deny . . .' White (1917), pp. 114–15; pp. 117–18
173   'One can't imagine . . .' Asquith (1968), pp. 445–8

POSTSCRIPT

177   'For several weeks . . .' Hayward (2001), pp. 37–84
178   'Tellingly . . .' Hayward (2001), p. 106

Bibliography

Asquith, Cynthia, *Diaries 1915–18*, Hutchinson, 1968

Aston, George, *Secret Service*, Faber & Faber, 1930

Baden-Powell, Olave, *Window on my Heart*, Hodder & Stoughton, 1973

Beaman, Ardern, *The Squadroon*, Bodley Head, 1920

Bertie, Lord Francis, *Diary 1914–18*, Hodder & Stoughton, 1924

Bland, J.O.P., *Germany's Violations of the Laws of War 1914–15*, William Heinemann, 1915

Bloem, Walter, *The Advance From Mons*, Peter Davies, 1930

Blunden, Edmund, *Undertones of War*, R. Cobden-Sanderson, 1928

Brittain, Vera, *Testament of Youth*, Gollancz, 1933

Buitenhuis, Peter, *The Great War of Words*, UBC Press, Vancouver, 1987

Callwell, Sir Charles, *Experiences of a Dug-Out 1914–18*, Constable, 1920

Charlton, William, *Arthur Machen*, The Richards Press, 1963

Charteris, John, *At GHQ*, Cassell, 1931

Churchill, Winston, *The World Crisis 1911–14*, Thornton Butterworth, 1923

Clark, Rev. Andrew, *Echoes of the Great War*, OUP, Oxford, 1985

Cockfield, Jamie, *With Snow on their Boots*, MacMillan, 1998

Cole, Christopher & Cheesman, E.F., *The Air Defence of Britain 1914–1918*, Putnam, 1984

Collins, L.J., *Theatre at War 1914–18*, MacMillan, 1998

Coppard, George, *With a Machine Gun to Cambrai*, IWM, 1980

Corbett-Smith, A., *The Retreat from Mons*, Cassell, 1916

——, *The Marne – And After*, Cassell, 1917

Dakers, Caroline, *The Countryside at War 1914–18*, Constable, 1987

Deacon, Richard, *British Secret Service*, Frederick Muller, 1969

Dudley, Ernest, *Monsters of the Purple Twilight*, Harrap, 1960

Edmonds, Sir J.E., *Military Operations – France & Belgium Vol 1*, British Official History, n.d.

Erzberger, Matthias, *Erlebnesse im Weltkrieg*, Stuttgart, 1920

Farrar, Martin, *News From the Front*, Sutton, 1998

Felstead, S.T., *German Spies at Bay*, Hutchinson, 1920

Fussell, Paul, *The Great War and Modern Memory*, OUP, Oxford, 1975

Gibbs, Philip, *Adventures in Journalism*, Heinemann, 1923

Gilbert, Martin, *The First World War*, Weidenfeld & Nicolson, 1994

Gillies, Midge, *Marie Lloyd*, Gollancz, 1999

Grant, Reginald, *SOS Stand To!*, D. Appleton, New York, 1918

Gray, Edwyn, *The U-Boat War*, Leo Cooper, 1994

Greene, Graham, *A Sort of Life*, Bodley Head, 1971

Griffith, Paddy (ed), *British Fighting Methods in the Great War*, Frank Cass, 1998

Haldane, Lord Richard, *Autobiography*, Hodder & Stoughton, 1929

Halpern, Paul, *A Naval History of World War One*, UCL Press, USA, 1994

Hammerton, Sir John (ed), *The Great War – I was There!*, Amalgamated Press, 1938

Hart, Basil Liddell, *The Real War*, Faber & Faber, 1930

Haste, Cate, *Keep the Home Fires Burning*, Allen Lane, 1977

Hay, Ian, *The First Hundred Thousand*, William Blackwood, Edinburgh, 1915

Haythornthwaite, Philip, *The WW1 Source Book*, Arms & Armour Press, 1992

Hayward, James, *The Bodies on the Beach*, CD41 Publishing, 2001

Hoare, Philip, *Wilde's Last Stand*, Duckworth, 1997

Horn, Pamela, *Rural Life in England in the First World War*, Gill & MacMillan, Dublin, 1984

Horne, John and Kramer, Alan, *German Atrocities 1914*, Yale University Press, 2001

Howe, Ellic, *The Black Game*, Michael Joseph, 1982

Kettle, Michael, *Salome's Last Veil*, Hart Davis & MacGibbon, 1977

Knightley, Phillip, *The First Casualty*, Quartet, 1982

Laffin, John, *British Butchers and Bunglers of World War One*, Sutton, 1988

Lomas, David, *Mons 1914*, Osprey, 1997

Lovat, Lord, *March Past*, Weidenfeld & Nicolson, 1978

McCrery, Nigel, *All the King's Men*, Simon & Schuster, 1992

McDonagh, Michael, *In London During the Great War*, Eyre & Spottiswoode, 1935

Macdonald, Lynne, *1914 – The Days of Hope*, Michael Joseph, 1987

Machen, Arthur, *The Bowmen & Other Legends of the War*, Simpkin, Marshall, Hamilton, Kent & Co, 1915

Mead, Gary, *The Doughboys*, Allen Lane, 2000

Messinger, Gary, *British Propaganda and the State in the First World War*, Manchester University Press, Manchester, 1992

Montagu, Ivor, *The Youngest Son*, Lawrence & Wishart, 1970

Montague, C.E., *Disenchantment*, Chatto & Windus, 1922

Morgan, J.H., *German Atrocities – An Official Investigation*, T. Fisher Unwin, 1916

Mosley, Oswald, *My Life*, Nelson, 1968

Neillands, Robin, *The Great War Generals on the Western Front 1914–18*, Robinson, 1997

Pankhurst, Sylvia, *The Home Front*, Hutchinson, 1932

Peat, Harold, *Private Peat*, Hutchinson, 1918

Peterson, H.C., *Propaganda for War*, University of Oklahoma Press, 1939

Playne, Caroline, *Society at War*, Allen & Unwin, 1931

Ponsonby, Lord Arthur, *Falsehood in Wartime*, Allen & Unwin, 1928

Read, Jamie Morgan, *Atrocity Propaganda 1914–19*, Yale University Press, USA, 1941

Reiss, R.A., *The Kingdom of Servia – Report*, Simpkin, Marshall, Hamilton, Kent & Co, 1916

Repington, Charles A'Court, *The First World War*, Constable, 1920

Reynolds, E.E., *B.P.*, Oxford University Press, Oxford, 1942

Richards, Frank, *Old Soldiers Never Die*, Faber, 1964

Richmond, Admiral Sir Herbert, *Diaries*, unpublished

Rimell, Raymond, *Zeppelin!*, Conway Maritime Press, 1984

Royle, Trevor, *Death Before Dishonour*, Mainstream, Edinburgh, 1982

Sanders, Michael and Taylor, Philip, *British Propaganda During the First World War*, Macmillan, 1982

Scott, Canon Frederick, *The Great War as I Saw It* [2nd Edition], Clarke & Stuart, Vancouver, 1934

Sellers, Leonard, *Shot in the Tower*, Leo Cooper, 1997

Sheffield, Gary, *Forgotten Victory*, Headline, 2001

Simpson, Colin, *Lusitania*, Longman, 1972

Sitwell, Osbert, *Laughter in the Next Room*, Macmillan, 1949

Stafford, David, *Churchill & Secret Service*, John Murray, 1997

Terraine, John, *Haig – The Educated Soldier*, Hutchinson, 1963

—, *The Smoke and the Fire*, Sidgwick & Jackson, 1980

—, *White Heat*, Sidgwick & Jackson, 1982

Thompson, Peter, *Lions Led by Donkeys*, T. Werner Laurie, 1927

Thomson, Basil, *Queer People*, Constable, 1922

Tippett, Maria, *Art at the Service of War*, Toronto University Press, 1984

Tomlinson, H.M., *Waiting for Daylight*, Cassell, 1922

Trumbo, Dalton, *Johnny Got His Gun*, New York, 1939

Turner, E.S., *Dear Old Blighty*, Michael Joseph, 1980

Viereck, George, *Spreading Germs of Hate*, Duckworth, 1931

Wallace, Graham, *Grahame-White*, Putnam & Co, 1960

Wemyss, Lady Wester, *The Life and Letters of Lord Wester Wemyss*, Eyre & Spottiswoode, 1935

West, Nigel, *MI5*, Bodley Head, 1981

White, Arnold, *The Hidden Hand*, Grant Richards, 1917

Whitehouse, Arch, *Heroes and Legends of WW1*, Doubleday, New York, 1964
Williams, John, *The Home Fronts*, Constable, 1972
Wilson, Trevor, *The Myriad Faces of War*, Polity Press, Cambridge, 1986

All titles published in London unless otherwise stated.

Articles
  Brooks, Richard, *The Great Myth of the First World War*, Military Illustrated, September 1998
McClure, Kevin, *Visions of Bowmen and Angels* (private printing, n.d.)
Ward, John, *Legend of murdered soldier lives on in bronze, Halifax Herald*, 22 July 2001

Archive Sources
  The official Canadian files on the Crucified Canadian legend are held by the National Archives of Canada in Ottawa, reference: RG25 (External Affairs), Series B1b, Volume 157, File C 12/71, 'Colonial Office (UK) Alleged Crucifixion of a Canadian Soldier by Germans, 1919'.

Index